Cambridge Elements ≡

Elements on Women in the History of Philosophy
edited by
Jacqueline Broad
Monash University

SUSAN STEBBING

Frederique Janssen-Lauret
University of Manchester

Shaftesbury Road, Cambridge CB2 8EA, United Kingdom

One Liberty Plaza, 20th Floor, New York, NY 10006, USA

477 Williamstown Road, Port Melbourne, VIC 3207, Australia

314–321, 3rd Floor, Plot 3, Splendor Forum, Jasola District Centre,
New Delhi – 110025, India

103 Penang Road, #05–06/07, Visioncrest Commercial, Singapore 238467

Cambridge University Press is part of Cambridge University Press & Assessment,
a department of the University of Cambridge.

We share the University's mission to contribute to society through the pursuit of
education, learning and research at the highest international levels of excellence.

www.cambridge.org
Information on this title: www.cambridge.org/9781009013031
DOI: 10.1017/9781009026925

First published 2022

A catalogue record for this publication is available from the British Library.

ISBN 978-1-009-01303-1 Paperback
ISSN 2634-4645 (online)
ISSN 2634-4637 (print)

Susan Stebbing

Elements on Women in the History of Philosophy

DOI: 10.1017/9781009026925
First published online: November 2022

Frederique Janssen-Lauret
University of Manchester

Author for correspondence: Frederique Janssen-Lauret,
frederique.janssen-lauret@manchester.ac.uk

Abstract: Susan Stebbing (1885–1943), the UK's first female professor of philosophy, was a key figure in the development of analytic philosophy. Stebbing wrote the world's first accessible book on the new polyadic logic and its philosophy. She made major contributions to the philosophy of science, metaphysics, philosophical logic, critical thinking, and applied philosophy. Nonetheless she has remained largely neglected by historians of analytic philosophy. This Element provides a thorough yet accessible overview of Stebbing's positive, original contributions, including her solution to the paradox of analysis, her account of the relation of sense-data to physical objects, and her anti-idealist interpretation of the new Einsteinian physics. Stebbing's innovative work in these and other areas helped move analytic philosophy from its early phase to its middle period.

Keywords: Stebbing, women in philosophy, history of analytic philosophy, logic, philosophy of science

ISBNs: 9781009013031 (PB), 9781009026925 (OC)
ISSNs: 2634-4645 (online), 2634-4637 (print)

Contents

1 Introduction: Susan Stebbing and Her Place in the History of Analytic Philosophy

Susan Stebbing was the UK's first female professor of philosophy as well as an anti-idealist philosopher of physics, an early advocate of mathematical logic, a pioneer of critical thinking, a trilingual anti-fascist activist, a secular humanist, and an educator of generations of female university students, the general public, and schoolchildren, including Jewish refugees. She deserves to be much better known than she is now. When Stebbing was born, in 1885, the fledgling cause of women's education was still highly controversial and under constant attack from the Victorian establishment. To attend a women's college, as Stebbing did when she went to Girton in 1903, was already a feminist act. To rise through the ranks as an academic even more so. By the time Stebbing reached her late forties, this was precisely what she had done. Her promotion to a professorial chair at Bedford College, a women's college in London, in 1933 inspired articles in several of the national newspapers. Advocates of women's education had prevailed, normalised the presence of women among university students, researchers, and holders of academic posts. And yet, although Stebbing was highly successful, she was and remained in many ways marginalised as a woman in academia.

All of Stebbing's publications from the 1920s onwards belong squarely to the tradition of analytic philosophy. Her contributions to the field were significant, and most were in the 'core' areas of analytic philosophy: logic, philosophy of science, and metaphysics. Stebbing wrote the world's first accessible book on the new symbolic logic and its philosophy (Stebbing, 1930), and a book on philosophy of physics containing a careful, measured rebuttal of idealistic interpretations pushed by prominent physicists (Stebbing, 1937). She published at least one paper per year in one of the major philosophy journals for most of her career, an unusual output for a philosopher in the early twentieth century. Stebbing was a pioneer in the field of critical thinking, publishing accessible books on good reasoning with a political slant in an effort to persuade the general public to spot the flaws in fascism. She co-founded the journal *Analysis* and introduced logical positivism to the British philosophical scene a few years before Ayer did (Stebbing, 1933b). During her lifetime, Stebbing held a relatively prominent position among British philosophers.

Her books were favourably reviewed and her papers well-received. She was chosen for prestigious roles in academia in the UK and abroad. She held a visiting professorship at Columbia, delivered the British Academy's annual lecture, and served as President of the Aristotelian Society. Nevertheless, she faced obstacles which her male counterparts did not have to contend with. She was turned down for a professorial chair at Cambridge because she was a woman at a time when Cambridge did not allow women to be members of the University. As a lecturer at a women's college, she had a high teaching load which was spread across most areas of philosophy. Women's colleges being underfunded and understaffed, her teaching load did not lessen after her promotion to Professor. Having been raised as a girl with a disability in the Victorian era, Stebbing had not received the rigorous training in classics and the exact sciences which her male counterparts took for granted. She had to embark on a self-education project in physics and its philosophy in her twenties and thirties. Had she had access to the educational resources in science, mathematics, and classics open to her colleagues G. E. Moore, Bertrand Russell, A. N. Whitehead, and Ludwig Wittgenstein, her contributions to logic and philosophy of science might have been greater still.

Despite her impressive achievements, Stebbing has also received little attention to date from historians of analytic philosophy. History of analytic philosophy, as we will discover shortly (Section 1.1), has often focussed exclusively on those men it unironically calls the 'founding fathers' of analytic philosophy, Moore, Russell, and Wittgenstein, and its 'grandfather', Gottlob Frege, sometimes to the point of outright identifying early analytic philosophy with the works of these 'forefathers' and analytic philosophy generally with these men and their followers. Such a narrow focus leaves no room for female founders, even ones as pivotal as Stebbing, nor for early analytic philosophers who were not followers of the 'Great Men', but critics or independent thinkers, no matter how analytic their work was thematically. Although some scholarly work on Stebbing has appeared in recent years, such work has often either been primarily biographical or tended to concentrate on her relationship to the canonical 'founding fathers' (Beaney, 2003, 2016; Milkov, 2003). An informative intellectual biography by Siobhan Chapman (2013) supplies a rich array of facts about Stebbing's life and her correspondence beyond what this short publication can cover but concentrates on Stebbing's life and on connections between her thought and contemporary thinking about ordinary language. By contrast, I will concentrate on giving a thorough yet accessible overview of Stebbing's positive, original contributions, including her views on the philosophy of logic (Section 2), her anti-idealist interpretation of the new Einsteinian physics (Section 3), her solution to the paradox of analysis (Section 4), and her pioneering work on critical thinking (Section 5). Although accessible, my overview of Stebbing's work is not in the style of a textbook or encyclopaedia piece. I defend original readings of Stebbing, take stances on interpretive issues, and provide support for the view that analytic philosophy should be regarded, not as the tradition of the followers and followers' followers of three or four Great Men but as a broad and varied movement with a variety of female and male ancestors, loosely unified by a focus on taking the methods and deliverances of the sciences as an inspiration for philosophy.

1.1 Early Analytic Philosophy, Stebbing's Role, and Historiography: Against the Great Men Narrative

Exactly when analytic philosophy began is a matter of dispute. Some historians argue it came into being as late as Wittgenstein's arrival in Cambridge to study with Russell in 1911 (Quinton, 2005: 28). Others, who consider Frege a founder, might say it began as early as his *Begriff-sschrift* (Frege, 1879). More commonly, historians consider Frege an ancestor rather than a founder of analytic philosophy (e.g. Burge, 2005: 7–8). Historians of this school of thought generally take the first work of analytic philosophy to be 'The Nature of Judgement' (Moore, 1899), the paper which inaugurated the mini-movement of two research fellows, Moore and Russell, dubbed by them 'The New Philosophy'. The New Philosophy was a fervently anti-idealist project. It went in search of a realist alternative to the idealism common in late nineteenth-century British universities, most pressingly to supplant the system of their key opponent, the British Hegelian F. H. Bradley (1883, 1897). The New Philosophers at first maintained that a view of judgement as a binary relation between a mind and something independent of and distinct from that mind meant that the logical form of true statements about judgement entailed the falsity of idealism (MacBride, 2018: 30–9). Moore and Russell's early attempts (Moore, 1899; Russell, 1903), which boldly suggested that all words refer, led to a bloated ontology and difficulties explaining the difference between truth and falsity. Attempts to rectify these shortcomings led to the theory of descriptions and logical atomism. Moore, Russell, and, a few years later, Wittgenstein (1922), replaced the faulty view that all words refer with the more viable proposal that it is instead every true sentence which stands for something – namely, for a fact. Falsity is then readily explained as failure to correspond to a fact. But our ordinary-language sentences do not straightforwardly map onto one fact each. They admit of further, detailed analysis. Logical atomism presumed that our claims about everyday middle-sized objects – humans, dogs, cats, plants, houses, cities, mountains, tables, and so on – were, strictly speaking, claims about a complex plurality of micro-facts: their components in some arrangement. A statement about a wooden table is really about protons and electrons arranged into atoms, which are in turn arranged into molecules, arranged into cells, arranged into cellulose fibres, arranged into planks, and arranged into the familiar tabular shape. We analyse statements about organisms into their physical (and perhaps mental) atoms in a biological arrangement.

Stebbing's most famous works were to focus on what exactly was involved in the process of analysis used in logical atomism and more generally in analytic philosophy. In several of her books and papers, she defended anti-idealism. It is readily apparent that her work concentrated on themes central to early analytic philosophy. Despite that fact, she has only rarely been considered a central figure in the analytic movement or a founder of analytic philosophy. Part of the explanation for her relative obscurity lies with gendered factors. Implicit and explicit sexist attitudes on the part of her contemporaries and of historians of analytic philosophy often led to a woman's works being cited less often and taken less seriously (Janssen-Lauret, in press-a). Institutional sexism meant that faculty at women's colleges had less visibility in the profession and less often succeeded at placing their former students in jobs where those students might promote the work of their former supervisors.

Stebbing has also been neglected because she has been given insufficient credit for originality. Ayer is typical in describing her as 'very much a disciple of Moore' (Ayer, 1977: 71). Several recent commentators also describe Stebbing several times over as a 'Moorean' (Milkov, 2003: 355, 358; Beaney, 2016: 242, 245–6, 248–50, 253–4; Beaney & Chapman, 2021: §§3–4). Although Stebbing certainly viewed Moore as a mentor figure, and regularly credited him with specific views she endorsed or with inspiring her to develop her own views on a given topic, she similarly gave credit to Russell and to Whitehead, on whose philosophy she wrote more papers than on Moore's (Stebbing, 1924, 1924–25, 1926). What's more, Stebbing's expertise stretched to technical areas of philosophy of which Moore never made any serious study. Moore's anti-idealism had originally grown out of rejecting the Kantianism he had found appealing as a young man and out of embracing the Platonism with which he had become familiar in his reading of the classics and his Moral Sciences degree. By contrast, Stebbing's anti-idealism found expression especially in her philosophical work on the new physics with its theory of relativity and subatomic particles. Unlike many of her contemporaries, Stebbing argued that the new physics did not obviously tell in favour of idealist or panpsychist interpretations. Stebbing also differed from Moore (but resembled Russell and Whitehead) in taking an interest in the philosophy of set theory. She discussed how modern mathematics affects ordinary-language discourse about numbers and the no-class theory (Stebbing, 1930: 141). Where Stebbing staked out a line in which she acknowledged the influence of Moore, as in her work on metaphysical analysis, she often made advances on his views, such as her sharp distinction between grammatical and directional analysis and her solution to the paradox of analysis (see Section 4). Stebbing further differed from Moore in the amount of attention she paid to usage in ordinary language. Chapman has presented an interpretation of Stebbing as making moves which foreshadowed modern discourse analysis and argumentation theory (Chapman, 2013: 172–86).

Stebbing, then, was also a clear representative of the branch of analytic philosophy which seeks to design a philosophy to fit the latest developments in mathematics and science. In this respect, she resembled Russell, Whitehead, or even W. V. Quine more than she resembled Moore. Stebbing is best seen as an original philosopher, a transitional figure who played a pivotal role in moving analytic philosophy on from its early phase, where (at least in the UK) it was dominated by logical atomism, towards a middle period typified by more focus on ordinary language and a more holist approach. To view her primarily as a Moorean is problematic because it denies her credit for originality, but also because it appears to fall prey to what I have called the Great Men narrative of analytic philosophy (Janssen-Lauret, in press-b). According to this historiographical narrative, analytic philosophy is the work of three or four particular men, their followers, and their followers' followers. Soames writes, 'analytic philosophy . . . is a certain historical tradition in which the early work of G. E. Moore, Bertrand Russell, and Ludwig Wittgenstein set the agenda for later philosophers' (Soames, 2003: xiii) and Beaney describes analytic philosophy as 'the tradition that originated in the work of Gottlob Frege (1848–1925), Bertrand Russell (1872–1970), G. E. Moore (1873–1958), and Ludwig Wittgenstein (1889–1951) and developed and ramified into the complex movement (or set of interconnected subtraditions) that we know today' (Beaney, 2013: 9).

Soames and Beaney's characterisations of analytic philosophy are formulated the way they are for a reason: to sidestep known issues with attempted definitions of 'analytic philosophy' which define it too narrowly, whether geographically as 'Anglo-American' philosophy, thematically as philosophy focussed on the analysis of language, or as 'critical' rather than speculative philosophy (Katzav & Vaesen, 2017). All of those candidate definitions leave out major figures in the history of analytic philosophy: German, Austrian, and Polish analytic philosophers, including Frege, Wittgenstein, Carnap, Tarski, Maria Kokoszynska, and Janina Hosiassion (Janssen-Lauret, 2022c); analytic metaphysicians like Russell, Stebbing, Moore, and Elizabeth Anscombe; and naturalistic system-builders such as Whitehead, Quine, Dorothy Emmet, and Mary Midgley.

But a definition of analytic philosophy as three or four men and their followers is overly narrow, too, not least because it misrepresents all women working on logic and philosophy of science in the early analytic period as either marginal figures who followed the Great Men or not analytic philosophers at all. The women whom I have dubbed 'grandmothers of analytic philosophy', including E. E. C. Jones and Christine Ladd-Franklin (Janssen-Lauret, in press-a, in in press-c),

Victoria Welby (Connell & Janssen-Lauret, 2022), and Grace de Laguna (Janssen-Lauret, in press-b) fall into the latter category. The 'grandmothers', similar in age to Frege or Whitehead rather than Russell or Wittgenstein, also resembled Frege in being originators of ideas – such as the sense-reference distinction (Jones, 1890) and inferentialism in logic and language which became influential only many years after the very early analytic period in which they lived. In recent work, Beaney has added Stebbing to his list as a fifth founder of analytic philosophy. While Beaney's solution is welcome in that it makes room for a female founder, it does not extend to grandparents of analytic philosophy other than Frege – notably, no grandmothers and no other candidate grandfathers like Whitehead or Stout (MacBride, 2018: 115–52) – nor for other analytic philosophers and logicians of similar stature to Stebbing, such as Carnap, Ramsey, and Tarski, who might lay equal claim to co-foundership.

My alternative proposal is to view analytic philosophy not as the works of some handful of individuals and their followers but rather as a broad and varied movement with a variety of strands, each with a range of central and more peripheral figures, each with doctrines in some respects allied, in some respects in tension with some of the others. There is no neat and tidy set of plausible necessary and sufficient conditions for who counts as an analytic philosopher or brief definition of 'analytic philosophy'. My model for the genesis of analytic philosophy is not that of the United States of America, a government of founding fathers gradually taking over land belonging to Indigenous peoples, or that of an exclusive gentlemen's club with a manifesto which sets the agenda for its followers. My models are, rather, those of wider intellectual, political, or artistic movements, a looser coalition of ideas, not all of which point in the same direction or are wholly mutually compatible. Among the strands making up the early analytic philosophy movement are empiricism, advances in formal and mathematical logic since the nineteenth-century revolution in rigour – not just Frege's but the algebraic calculi, too – the analysis of language, and new developments in physics and psychology. On that alternative conception of analytic philosophy, it has multiple grandfathers and grandmothers besides Frege and multiple founding fathers and mothers, too. One way to restore female early analytic philosophers to their rightful place is to give up the hero narrative of the Great Men and embrace the 'movement' narrative of early analytic philosophy.

What I take to be most distinctive about early analytic philosophy is its quest to find a philosophy compatible with new developments in the sciences, especially the natural sciences and pure mathematics. Most narratives of the emergence of analytic philosophy to date have focussed more on early Russell and Moore's opposition to idealism (e.g. Hylton, 1990; Candlish, 2007). But Frege, Russell, Whitehead, and other early analytic philosophers were also driven by reflection on the mathematical revolution in rigour and general relativity. These results upset traditional philosophical certainties about the infinite, parts and wholes – for example, the intuition that no whole is the same size as any of its proper parts – and the nature of space and time. Analytic philosophers held that philosophy should accept these results as true, set out to clarify and interpret them, and fit philosophical enquiry around them (MacBride & Janssen-Lauret, 2015). For some lesser-known early or proto-analytic philosophers, such as Welby, Stout, Ladd-Franklin, and de Laguna, reflection on new findings in the emerging science of psychology was also a major driving force. A further concern for many early analytic philosophers was opposition to idealism, although later generations of analytic philosophers contained some idealists. Critical analysis of linguistic meaning, reference, and truth became crucial items in the analytic philosopher's toolbox as she set out to investigate the logical form of scientific truths and their collective ontological commitments. Stebbing, as we shall see, was an exemplar of analytic philosophy in her careful analysis of the logical forms of both physics and ordinary language. She was also typical of early analytic philosophy in her anti-idealism, although she, initially inspired by idealist philosophy as a student, was a reasonably sympathetic reader of idealism and anxious to represent idealist solutions fairly in her philosophy of physics. Lastly, Stebbing, sensitive to ordinary language and always clear that analytic philosophers must analyse sentences, can be seen as a transitional figure in the shift from logical atomism – which speaks of analysing propositions and tends to treat language as a 'transparent' (Russell, 1926: 118) medium to which we need not pay attention – towards the middle phase of analytic philosophy with its increasing focus on ordinary language.

1.2 Susan Stebbing: Life, Works, and Historical Context

Born in London in 1885 and orphaned in her teens, Susan Stebbing's pre-university education consisted largely of intermittent homeschooling. Stebbing was not merely a Victorian girl-child – already at a disadvantage with respect to educational opportunities – but also significantly disabled by Ménière's disease, an inner-ear disorder which causes attacks of dizziness and nausea and was not, at the time, treatable. Stebbing's disability, and probably her lack of rigorous training in the exact sciences and the classics, limited her choice of subjects at Girton College, where the logician E. E. Constance Jones, one of the grandmothers of analytic philosophy, had recently been appointed Mistress. Stebbing began by reading History. According to different sources (Wisdom, 1944: 283; Chapman, 2013: 11) she might have preferred either Classics or Natural Sciences. Perhaps her disability was incompatible with work in a laboratory. But there may also have been gendered pressures nudging her away from natural sciences and classics, which were, in the 1900s, among the most strongly male-coded fields in the academy.

The Victorian and Edwardian doctrine of gendered 'separate spheres' relegated women to the home, leaving the public sphere to men (this will be explored more in Section 2). Belief in separate spheres led many Victorians to oppose higher education for women altogether but disposed others to allow for higher education which did not require worldly knowledge potentially affecting women's moral respectability. As a result, late Victorian and Edwardian culture did not classify all of mathematics as strongly masculine. Applied mathematics, used in the physical sciences and engineering, fields associated with economic gain and the public sphere, was highly male-coded. But those who didn't wholly disapprove of women's education often considered pure mathematics, such as mathematical logic, algebra, and set theory, which did not draw on worldly knowledge, suitable for a woman to study. For example, Grace Chisholm's mathematics lecturers advised her to leave the very applied department in Cambridge to pursue her PhD in pure geometry in Germany (Jones, 2000). Christine Ladd-Franklin was encouraged to give up trying to persuade reluctant male physics professors to admit her to their research laboratories and instead pursue pure mathematics, which she could study at home (Janssen-Lauret, in press-a). Limited instruction in the classics was another frequent obstacle for the early generations of female academics. Educated parents immersed their sons in Greek and Latin from early childhood but only rarely did the same for their daughters. Constance Jones recounted in her autobiography that the women of her family learnt only enough Latin to teach their sons until the boys went to school (Jones, 1922: 11). Even in the early 1940s, Mary Warnock and her fellow female classics students found 'what a struggle it was for girls to keep their heads above water in Mods, an examination based on the assumption that boys had been learning Latin and Greek almost as soon as their education had started' (Warnock, 2000: 39).

Towards the end of her history degree, Stebbing happened at random upon Bradley's *Appearance and Reality* while browsing in the library. She was immediately gripped. Stebbing decided to stay at Girton for another year to read for the Moral Sciences Tripos, as Cambridge called its exams in philosophy. She studied philosophy with the logician W. E. Johnson, who introduced her to Aristotelian logic. But Cambridge did not allow women who passed their Tripos exams to graduate with their degrees and would not begin to do so until 1948, after Stebbing's death. Stebbing accordingly moved to the University of London, which did award degrees to women.

In London, she completed a master's thesis on truth, pragmatism, and the French voluntarism of Bergson, later published in the Girton series by Cambridge University Press (Stebbing, 1914). After her move to London in the early 1910s, Stebbing continued to teach for Girton on a casual basis, as well as for Newnham, another Cambridge women's college. She also held visiting lectureships in London, at King's College for Women, and Homerton, a teacher training college. Stebbing regularly spoke at the Aristotelian Society and published papers in its *Proceedings*. Several of these earliest publications of hers were sympathetic to idealism. In one meeting of the Society, Stebbing criticised Russell's views on relations and, though also disinclined to follow Bradley all the way down the road to monism, defended the idealist doctrine of concrete unity (Stebbing, 1916–17). Some twenty-five years later, Stebbing recounted that, having presented her paper, she was confronted about the 'muddles' (a favourite word of hers) inherent in her claims by a man she later discovered to be G. E. Moore. Stebbing described feeling 'alarmed' at first at Moore's 'thumping the table' as he asked, repeatedly, 'What on earth do you mean by that?', but being soon drawn into the substance of the discussion to such an extent that she forgot to feel alarmed or apprehensive: '[N]othing mattered except trying to find out what I did mean', she wrote (Stebbing, 1942: 530).

Although Stebbing commentators often make much of her labelling her first encounter with Moore as a 'conversion' (Chapman, 2013: 34; Beaney, 2016: 242; Beaney & Chapman, 2021: §3), it should be borne in mind that its context is a paper which is both explicitly intended as a homage to Moore and written by Stebbing in a retrospective mood, as her own health was failing. A closer look at the historical evidence reveals that Stebbing's 'conversion' appears to have been both more gradual than the quotation suggests and a conversion to analytic philosophy generally rather than a conversion to 'Moorean' philosophy. First, Stebbing wrote and presented a second paper critical of Moore soon afterwards, accusing him of a 'misuse of terms' and of making 'a serious mistake, viz. . . . the identification of reality with existence' (Stebbing, 1917–18: 583). Chapman notes that Stebbing and Moore engaged in a frank exchange of views in correspondence afterwards (Chapman, 2013: 34–5). Stebbing then published few original philosophical papers for a few years. Her philosophical thought was possibly in flux, but it is also known that she was busy with other professional activities. She was searching for an academic job, while at the same time setting up a girls' school, Kingsley Lodge, with her sister Helen and her friends Hilda Gavin and Vivian Shepherd, as well as engaging in anti-war activism in the form of lectures on behalf of the League of Nations Union, advocating disarmament (Chapman, 2013: 37–8). In 1920, Stebbing finally secured one of the few and far between academic posts open to women, a lectureship at Bedford College, a women's college in London. From 1924 to 1929, Stebbing published a flurry of serious, original journal papers clearly belonging to the tradition of analytic philosophy. But these were not works of Moorean common-sense philosophy. Stebbing spent most of the 1920s publishing extensively on philosophy of physics, a topic which had been of interest to her since at least her master's thesis, which includes detailed discussions of the question of whether physical laws are necessary (Stebbing, 1914: 3, 28–35, 70–1). Her main interlocutors were the analytic philosopher and logician A. N. Whitehead, the idealist physicist Arthur Eddington, and to a lesser extent other analytic figures such as Bertrand Russell, C. D. Broad, and C. E. M. Joad and other idealist physicists such as James Jeans. Moore, immersed in the classics to an extraordinary degree from his schooldays, and whose early philosophy had been inspired by Plato, with Kant and Bradley as foils, never made any serious venture into the philosophy of physics. We will examine Stebbing's philosophy of physics in Section 3. Stebbing clearly regarded Moore as a mentor figure and mentioned him regularly in her work on incomplete symbols and analysis, which dates mostly from the early 1930s. Stebbing was generous with acknowledgements where she took her views to originate with others, a trait typical of early analytic female philosophers (Connell & Janssen-Lauret, 2022). Although this trait is, in general, admirable, Stebbing at times gave herself insufficient credit for originality. In Section 4, I will argue that her theory of analysis in fact makes a significant advance on Moore's, despite Stebbing's modesty about her own achievements relative to his.

Stebbing enjoyed great success in her career at Bedford College. She was promoted to the position of being the UK's first female professor of philosophy in 1933. She published primarily on philosophy of science, formal and philosophical logic, metaphysics, and language, including the first accessible book on the new symbolic logic, *A Modern Introduction to Logic*. Stebbing continued to suffer severe attacks of Ménière's disease but used these periods of illness to read books in English, French, and German, often publishing her thoughts as a book review. As a result of her extensive reading and trilingualism, Stebbing was one of the first outside of continental Europe to see the significance of logical positivism. She published a detailed study of the movement (Stebbing, 1933b) three years before Ayer published his *Language, Truth, and Logic*. Stebbing's publications on logical positivism did much to introduce it to the British philosophical scene. In the late 1930s, Stebbing, increasingly alarmed by the rise of fascism and generally conscious that the general public would benefit from the ability to detect and resist fallacious argumentation and manipulative uses of language by those in authority, began to write on the application of critical thinking to ethics and politics. She also worked with Jewish refugees, work which she continued until her death in 1943.

2 Logic

Susan Stebbing seems always to have loved logic and to have felt at home within it. As a Girton undergraduate, she had studied Aristotelian logic with W. E. Johnson, who would later write, with significant help and support from Newnham philosophy student Naomi Bentwich (Johnson, 1924: v), a three-volume magnum opus entitled *Logic*. The mistress of Girton, E. E. Constance Jones, was herself a logician, then author of three books (Jones, 1980, 1982, 1905). We know that Stebbing and Jones discussed logic together, too, because Jones thanked Stebbing for helping her with the proofs of the second edition of her *Primer of Logic* (Jones, 1913: i). Among Stebbing's early publications, before she became an analytic philosopher, is a defence of (Aristotelian) logic against the charge that it is mostly useless in everyday reasoning (Stebbing, 1915).

Twenty-first-century Western readers may feel a sense of surprise at seeing several logicians among the first and second generations of UK and US women to enter higher education and specialise in philosophy. The contemporary stereotype is that women in philosophy, who remain a small minority within the field, prefer moral or political philosophy to logic. In our late twentieth- and early twenty-first-century Western cultural context, logic is associated with masculinity. But this association of male thinkers with logic and female thinkers with normative philosophy, I will show, is a relatively recent invention, not common in the days of early analytic philosophy. All women who held academic jobs in philosophy in the United States or the UK, and many on the European continent, prior to the 1940s of whom I'm aware were experts either on logic broadly conceived or on history of philosophy. Some also published on normative philosophy; some did not. Besides Jones and Stebbing, in the 1890s–1910s Christine Ladd-Franklin, Sophie Bryant, Mary Everest Boole, Constance Naden, Margaret Floy Washburn, Mary Whiton Calkins, Beatrice Edgell, Augusta Klein, Grace de Laguna, and Helen Dendy also published regularly in mainstream philosophy journals on formal logic, philosophical logic, and the application of logic to other fields such as psychology. Notable female historians of philosophy include Elizabeth Haldane, the Descartes scholar and translator, and M. J. Levett, the celebrated translator of the *Theaetetus*.

But I have found no women employed in anglophone academic philosophy posts before the late 1940s who published only on normative philosophy.

Other early analytic philosophers, male and female, also regularly described their female colleagues as especially good at or interested in logic, without indicating that they found anything odd about this. A paper on Ladd-Franklin's logical system, for example, rhapsodised, 'No scheme in logic that has ever been proposed is more beautiful than that . . . of Dr. Ladd-Franklin' (Shen 1927: 54; see also Janssen-Lauret, in press-a). Stout wrote in his obituary of Jones, 'Logic . . . was her special subject, and it is only here that she would herself have made any claim to originality' (Stout, 1922: 383). It was not merely pro-feminist men interested in logic who described women as such. Even a patronising and facetious reply to Stebbing's 1915 paper by a detractor of logic, which speaks of acting 'out of deference to Miss Stebbing's sex' and not wanting 'to hurt Miss Stebbing's feelings' (Mercier, 1915: 19), nevertheless refers to her repeatedly as 'a logician' (Mercier, 1915: 18, 20) and deplores the way her 'exceptional mental power' has been 'corroded and attenuated by the study of logic'. Though quite openly sexist, Mercier nevertheless appears to see no tension between Stebbing's identity as a woman and her identity as a logician.

All academic fields were of course male-dominated in the late Victorian and Edwardian period in which Stebbing grew up and first attended Girton, during which women's education remained a controversial cause. Women had to make heroic efforts to be accepted even as second-class colleagues by male academics. Men routinely disparaged women's intellectual abilities. But the strongest bulwarks of masculinity within the academy were not logic, philosophy, or pure mathematics. In these fields, we see several notable female scholars, like Constance Jones, Christine Ladd-Franklin, and Grace Chisholm Young, embarking on academic careers from the 1880s onwards. Classics as an academic field and politics as a field and an activity were much more strongly male-coded in late Victorian and Edwardian Western European and North American society. The doctrine of gendered 'separate spheres', which was prevalent in those societies, claimed that women's sphere was the home, as a safe haven from man's inherent aggression and competitiveness and associated with moral virtues of peacefulness, piety, and purity (Laslett & Brenner, 1989: 387). Men ruled the public sphere, which included higher education as well as politics and the marketplace, a sphere decidedly less shot through with moral virtue and imbued with the kind of worldly knowledge from which women were shielded. Although I shall concentrate on Stebbing's largely white and upper/middle-class British context, I note that cultural variations existed. In particular, some ethnic minority groups within Western societies, such as African American communities, largely adhered to Victorian ideals of domesticity but highly prized women's education (Carlson, 1992: 61–2), and working-class communities of all ethnic groups valued women's paid work outside the home, which they did not view as being at odds with domesticity (Laslett & Brenner, 1989: 389).

Politics, academic and practical, was described as an essentially masculine enterprise, especially by opponents of women's suffrage. Anti-suffragists seized upon the doctrine of separate spheres to argue that involvement in politics would erode women's pure, instinctive virtue. They justified their opposition to women's suffrage on the grounds that women were not suited to politics because emotion, not reason, informed women's morality. Anti-feminists argued that while feminine, instinctive morality was well-suited to child-rearing and the domestic sphere, it had no role to play in the cold, calculating world of politics, where women would invariably 'consider personalities above principles' when they cast their votes or became involved in governing (Hopkins, 1913: 8). According to the doctrine of separate spheres, women's moral superiority did not issue from rational reflection or knowledge of ethical theory. It flowed from motherly love, self-sacrifice, and domesticity. Western Victorian and Edwardian cultural mores mostly did not encourage women to study or teach moral theory in colleges or universities. And they viewed women as outright incompetent in the realm of politics, a competitive field drawing upon quite unfeminine worldly knowledge. Logic, by contrast, whether Aristotelian or mathematical, could be studied from home or entirely within the safe walls of a women's college. As a result, it was considered, by those who approved of women's higher education but upheld separate spheres, as a safe subject for a woman to study.

Female logicians in fact made key contributions to logic in the late nineteenth century. Formal logic, which had long been considered a fully finished science, completed by Aristotle and no longer subject to development (Kant, 1787, Bviii), was beginning to be revised in light of novel developments in nineteenth-century science and mathematics. Empiricist logicians like Mill (1843) and Venn recognised an inductive branch of logic alongside the deductive. Constance Naden's book on the subject, *Induction and Deduction* (Naden, 1890), was described by a sexist reviewer as displaying 'a power of acute reasoning such as few other women have ever possessed' (Ω, 1891: 292). Mathematically inclined logicians began to apply algebraic methods to syllogistic logic. One of the major figures in this tradition was Christine Ladd-Franklin, who reconceptualised Aristotelian logic as a calculus based on the relation of exclusion, effectively a NAND-operator (Ladd, 1883; Ladd-Franklin, 1889, 1911, 1912; see also Uckelman, 2021; Janssen-Lauret, in press-a). Ladd-Franklin in addition had an excellent eye for natural-language illustrations of logical principles used in everyday reasoning: 'When I said to my little girl, "I will take you down town this afternoon if you are good," she said "And only?" – meaning: That is no doubt a sufficient condition, but is it also indispensable?"' (Ladd-Franklin, 1912: 646). Ladd-Franklin was highly regarded by her contemporaries. Whitehead, in his *Universal Algebra*, cited Ladd-Franklin, not Frege, for the latest work on quantification and existence assumptions (Whitehead, 1898: 116). Venn highly praised the 1883 published version of her PhD (Venn, 1883: 595–601). Constance Jones made a major advance in philosophical logic when she queried the third of the traditional Aristotelian Laws of Thought, the Law of Identity. Jones denied that subject-predicate statements in general express identities, as most are not of the logical form 'A is A'. According to Jones, their logical form is, rather, one which states 'an identity of denomination in diversity of attribution' (Jones, 1890: 46), that is, they attribute to the same referent two different properties, using phrases with different 'significations' (Jones, 1892: 20). Jones, then, proposed with what she called her 'New Law of Thought' or 'analysis of categoricals', a version of what we now know as the sense-reference distinction and was described as such by her contemporaries: 'a theory expressed first by Miss

Constance Jones as long ago as 1890, and, a little later, by Prof. Frege'
(Klein, 1911: 521).

2.1 Stebbing's Views on Logic

Stebbing was the author of the first accessible book on the new, symbolic logic. Her *Modern Introduction to Logic* (Stebbing, 1930, 1933a)
is often described as a 'text-book', but although Stebbing's intended
audience was students, to speak of a logic 'text-book' is apt to con-
jure up, for the twenty-first-century reader, an image of a short book,
focussed on exercises for students, which details the views of others
without originality. Stebbing's book, by contrast, was a 500-page behe-
moth, taking in Western formal and philosophical logic from Aristotle
to Russell and Whitehead's *Principia Mathematica* and Wittgenstein's
Tractatus, in which Stebbing frequently defended original philosophical
viewpoints of the sort we would now expect to find in a monograph.
A short publication like this one permits only a whistle-stop tour of
Stebbing's philosophy of logic (see also Janssen-Lauret, 2017, 2022a;
Douglas & Nassim, 2021). As we shall see, Stebbing expressed original
views on logicality – the question what makes a theory logic – where she
emphasised the importance of formality conceived as universal applicability; on the nature of logical consequence, where she advocated for
material consequence; and on the continuity between logic and scientific
methodology, which she viewed in hypothetico-deductive terms. Stebbing's best-known contribution to logic pertains to her views on analysis,
logical constructions, and incomplete symbol theory, which I will cover
first.

Stebbing's innovations in the theory of philosophical analysis also
inform her metaphysics and, I argue in what follows, her philosophy
of science. Her work on logic and its role in facilitating philosophical analysis stressed that what philosophers analyse is language, not
propositions or judgments, that the logical form of a sentence is context-
dependent, and that logical construction needs careful definition. This
work prepared the way for her celebrated distinction between grammatical or same-level analysis – analysis of language in terms of a further
stretch of language, which may be analytic or a priori – and metaphysical or directional analysis, which specifies what simple elements in what

configuration there are in the world in case the sentence is true (see Section 4).

To appreciate the novelty of Stebbing's contributions, we need a brief sketch of the historical backdrop, beginning with how Stebbing's predecessors, especially Moore and Russell but also Constance Jones, reacted to those authors whom Stebbing labelled the 'traditional logicians'. Stebbing's 'traditional logicians' included the idealists Bosanquet and Bradley, whose logic was Aristotelian but, by Stebbing's lights, had lost sight of the most positive features of Aristotle's thought, the formalism which Aristotle shared with mathematical logic (Stebbing, 1930: x–xii) by mistakenly setting 'form' in opposition to 'Reality' and proposing instead a 'metaphysical logic' governed by the principle of 'identity-in-diversity'.

Russell and Moore's first venture into anti-idealism, the New Philosophy, had rebelled against idealism, with Bradley as their main foil. According to Bradley's (and Bosanquet's) identity-in-diversity view, what we think of as ordinary identity claims or subject-predicate statements never represent reality correctly. Bradley and Bosanquet claimed that true identity between subject and predicate could not be asserted due to the 'difference in meaning' (Bradley, 1883: 28), that we 'cannot speak of the coincident part as the same, except by an ideal synthesis which identifies it first with one of the two outlines and then with the other' (Bosanquet, 1888: 358). Bradley maintained that our thoughts and language must always radically misrepresent reality, because reality is fundamentally one, completely without structure. By contrast, thought and language are composed of parts and concatenated with a definite structure in order to represent. Rejection of the Bradley–Bosanquet line does not require rejection of Aristotelian syllogistic logic. Constance Jones, who adhered in the main to Aristotelian formal logic despite replacing one of its covering laws with her New Law of Thought, had already raised the worry that Bradley's view 'seems to me to depend on a confusion between identity and similarity' (Jones, 1890: 50 n.1). The young Moore (1899, 1900–01) and Russell (1903: §46) did not initially take Jones's sensible way out; Jones expressed polite puzzlement that Moore, in 1900, fell into the same mistake as Bosanquet of running together qualitative and quantitative identity, when they are easily distinguished in ordinary language (Jones, 1900–01; see also

Janssen-Lauret, in press-c). Rather, Moore and Russell at first responded by offering, instead of the idealist modus ponens – if reality does not resemble our thoughts and language, then we cannot represent it correctly, and reality indeed fails to resemble our thoughts and language – a modus tollens: our thoughts and language certainly can represent reality correctly. Therefore reality does resemble our thoughts. Each of our words is a symbol complete in itself, whose task is to refer to some component of reality. Reality does divide into parts, and our minds can reach out and grasp, and name, components of reality directly. This 'all-words-refer' model ran aground. It made it impossible to make non-existence claims and to distinguish true statements from false ones.

The mathematical, symbolic logic which Russell increasingly turned to, having first read Frege in 1902, provided a basis to solve the New Philosophers' problems. In short, they moved to a model on which it is not the case that every word stands for something but every true proposition (or judgement) does stand for something, namely for a fact. Falsity, then, is the property a proposition or judgement has when it fails to stand for a fact. Russell used symbolic logic and its theory of quantification to account for falsity and negative existentials. Symbolic logic had grown out of new developments in nineteenth-century mathematics, the revolution in rigour which made mathematicians turn their attention to their deductive proof methods. Previously, logicians and mathematicians had been content to build their systems up from principles which appeared to them to be intuitively true. But intuition proved no fit guide for mathematicians exploring novel systems, like Cantor's theory of transfinite numbers, and the new theory of classes, which introduced higher and lower levels of infinity. Mathematicians' only guide was adherence to clearly laid-out proof methods. Instead of relying on syllogistic forms, where each premise or conclusion has just one quantifier, rigorous new treatments of arithmetic and geometry also needed statements with multiple quantifiers, such as 'for each number, there is another number which is its successor' or 'in between any two points on a line, there is another point'. They needed a polyadic (that is, multiple-quantifier) logic, like Frege's *Begriffsschrift* (1879). Frege thought of his quantifiers as higher-order properties: to say that so-and-sos exist is to say that the so-and-so property has instances. Russell put such quantifiers to work in accounting for negative existentials. A negative existential proposition does not single out, say, a unicorn and say of it that it does not exist; the proposition says that there are no instances of the unicorn property.

Where the early Russell–Moore view had assumed that all words are complete symbols, whose only function is to refer, their new, improved model introduced incomplete symbols, whose function is different. Their contribution to meaning is revealed through analysis. Russell focussed in particular on definite descriptions, which look, grammatically, like they stand for some component of reality but whose grammatical form misleads us. Although 'the present Queen of France is an equestrian' looks very similar to the true statement 'the present Queen of England is an equestrian', it is neither true that the present Queen of France is an equestrian nor that she never rides, because there is no present Queen of France. Russell's solution was to say that 'the present Queen of France' is not referential. It is a disguised quantifier phrase, which disappears upon analysis: 'The proposition "a is the so-and-so" means that a has the property so-and-so, and nothing else has' (Russell, 1910–11: 113). Proper names, complete symbols, stand for constituents of propositions known to us directly. Definite descriptions, by contrast, have no meaning in isolation, so their function is not referential. They do not introduce a referent as the constituent of a proposition; they say of a property that it has exactly one instance. Descriptions, definite or indefinite, are useful in explaining that non-existence claims do not ascribe the property of non-existence to a constituent of a proposition but amount to the assertion that it is not the case that exactly one thing has the so-and-so property. They also help us account for falsity. A false proposition is likewise an incomplete symbol, which arranges words in a way in which nothing is arranged in the world.

It is not just 'the present Queen of France', but also 'the present Queen of England', which is an incomplete symbol according to Russell. Assuming that the reader is not personally acquainted with the Queen, they know her only by description: they know that there is presently one unique instance of the Queen-of-England property. Even those acquainted with the Queen are acquainted only with a visible surface of her – her face, for example, not the back of her head – at a specific time. Although they know that she otherwise exists as a complex arrangement of mental and physical states, they know this descriptively, not directly. The Queen is, to them, a logical construct, or, as Russell sometimes said, a logical *fiction*, someone whose existence and nature we know of through descriptive knowledge of her properties. Russell's mature view at this time preserved the assumption, so central to his and Moore's first venture into anti-idealism, that our minds can reach out and grasp, and name, constituents of reality directly.

Complete symbols or proper names, encoding in language a sign of immediate acquaintance with something in the world, remained. Russell stressed that we need them, as they are where analysis terminates: 'Every proposition which we can understand must be composed wholly of constituents with which we are acquainted' (Russell, 1910–11: 117). On Russell's view, analysis terminates in 'sense-data'. Although sense-data are now generally thought of as mental states, such an account of them is not necessary. Moore considered an interpretation on which sense-data are identical with the surfaces of objects (Moore, 1925: 59). Russell at times admitted acquaintance with universals and the self, not merely with mental states.

Stebbing enthusiastically embraced incomplete symbol theory for its potential to account for negative existentials. Stebbing considered it 'plain common sense' that 'negative existential propositions are true if there is no individual in the actual world to which the descriptive phrase applies' (Stebbing, 1930: 56). She also mentioned negative existentials as playing an important role in science. She contrasted the planet Neptune, posited to explain irregularities in the orbit of Uranus, and subsequently observed, thus confirming the hypothesis, with the positing of the planet Vulcan to explain irregularities in the orbit of Mercury. Vulcan was never observed, because there is no such planet. The irregularities in Mercury's orbit are explained instead by Einsteinian general relativity (Stebbing, 1930: 346, 398). While Stebbing also embraced the project of logical construction, she sought to improve on Russell's version of it.

One feature of Stebbing's thought which sets it apart from that of Russell and Moore is her insistence that what philosophers analyse is not propositions, judgements, or things themselves but language, and specifically sentences or other expressions used on some occasion, in some context. The early Russell had explicitly held the view that 'symbols were always, so to speak, transparent', that is, that language is a medium we need not pay attention to, whose only job is to stand for something outside itself. In *Principia*, an occurrence of a term is called 'referentially transparent' iff nothing is said of it but by means of it something is said of something else (Whitehead & Russell, 1964 [1910]: appendix C). Stebbing was among the first to stress the importance of context in interpreting occurrences of expressions, as Quine was also to do in his development of referential transparency (Quine, 1953: 124). But neither of them was the first to do so. Russell admitted that he had first seen a rebuttal of the transparency of language in 'Lady Welby's work on the subject, but failed to take it seriously' (Russell, 1926: 118).

Stebbing argued that Russell's claim that 'the proposition "a is the so-and-so" means that a has the property so-and-so, and nothing else has' is not independent of context because some sentences of the form 'a is the so-and-so' do not contain definite descriptions. For example, 'the whale is a mammal' is usually used to express a taxonomical claim about whales and has the form of a universal generalisation, equivalent to 'all whales are mammals'. A sentence such as 'the dog is fond of peanut butter' is ambiguous. It can be used to make a generalisation about all dogs, in which case it is a universal generalisation, or to make a statement about a particular dog, identified by context (I might say it about my dog Daphne; Stebbing might have said it about her dog Smoodger), in which case it contains an incomplete symbol. Stebbing thus recommended a refined account of incomplete symbols, which she credited to Moore in correspondence, '"S, in this usage, is an incomplete symbol" = "S, in this usage, does occur in expressions which express propositions, and in the case of every such expression, S never stands for any constituent of the proposition expressed"' (Stebbing, 1930: 155). Stebbing credited her criticisms of Russell on incomplete symbols to the influence of Moore, in discussions and correspondence with him rather than his published work. But there are some potential signs that Stebbing was overly modest here, and her view is more original than it appears. It is notable, for example, that Moore consistently spoke of the objects of analysis as propositions (e.g. Moore, 1925; see also Section 4 in this Element). By contrast, even in 1930 Stebbing's criticisms already clearly turn on thinking of analysis as analysis of language: 'in logical analysis there are not two *things* but two *expressions* which mean the same' (Stebbing, 1930: 441).

Stebbing criticised Russell for speaking loosely about logical constructions. She took exception to his calling them 'fictions' and not distinguishing between incomplete symbols – which are expressions of language – and logical constructions, as, for example, when he wrote, 'classes are, in fact, like descriptions, logical fictions, or (as we say) "incomplete symbols" ' (Russell, 1919: 181–2), a line Stebbing described as 'extremely confused' (Stebbing, 1930: 157). She also expressed hesitation about Russell's claim that a definition in mathematics is the 'expression of a volition' – 'a declaration that a certain newly-introduced symbol or combination of symbols is to mean the same as a certain other combination of symbols of which the meaning is already known' (Whitehead & Russell, 1964 [1910]: Introduction). Stebbing here took Russell to be running together defining on the one hand, which is a relation between expressions, with analysis of concepts on the other hand. Unlike definition, conceptual analysis takes the form of stating which properties are conjoined in a given concept. Stebbing maintained, first of all, that definitions were relations between expressions but not merely syntactic items. Rather, 'the definiendum and the definiens express the same referend' (Stebbing, 1930: 441), that is, they stand for the same thing. Similarly, Stebbing maintained that a mathematical definition can elucidate a concept but is not a definition of the concept. It 'marks an advance in knowledge' rather than telling us only what we already knew (Stebbing, 1930: 441).

Stebbing maintained from early in her career that, if logical construction theory was true and useful, it had to be defined in terms of incomplete symbol theory. As Russell had provided only examples and no definition, Stebbing proposed one: she defined 'Any X is a logical construction' as 'X is symbolised by "S" and "an S" is an incomplete symbol' (Stebbing, 1930: 157). In 1930, Stebbing said little about her own original views concerning logical construction theory, which may indicate that at that time she was hesitant to endorse it fully. Although she felt able to declare that classes were logical constructions (Stebbing, 1930: 455), she seemed less certain about macro-physical objects. She raised a worry that, if macro-physical objects such as lions are logical constructions, then lions turn out not to be particulars (Stebbing, 1930: 159 n.2); only sense-data are to be counted as particulars on such a view.

By the second edition of her book (Stebbing, 1933a), Stebbing had come around to a firmer, and original, view on logical construction theory. She added to the discussions above an appendix providing a clear statement of the view that 'there are good reasons for supposing that . . . persons are logical constructions' (Stebbing, 1933a: 502; see also Stebbing, 1933a: 146 n.1). Stebbing remained resolutely opposed to calling logical constructions 'fictions' and hesitant about the nomenclature of 'logical construction', 'for it suggests that something is constructed, which is not the case . . . to say that the table is a logical fiction (or construction) is not to say that the table is a fictitious, or imaginary, object; it is rather to deny that, in any ordinary sense, it is an object at all' (Stebbing, 1933a: 502). Stebbing's position on logical construction differed from Russell's. Unlike Russell, Stebbing did not hold that analysis terminates in sense-data, nor that we can name sense-data. In the sections that follow on Stebbing's philosophy of science and metaphysics, we will see Stebbing's reasons for dispensing with sense-data and substituting observations, or perceptual objects.

In short, Stebbing saw no need to require that analysis terminates in something which 'Russell . . . could regard as an indubitable datum' (Stebbing, 1933a: 503). According to Stebbing, analysis need not terminate in indubitable data, or objects of acquaintance (see also Section 4). In another paper in the same year, Stebbing also cast doubt on Russell's contention that our language allows for pure reference without any discursive content: 'Ordinary language is essentially descriptive. It is for this reason that no non-general fact can be expressed. If we attempted to use a sentence not containing any descriptive symbol, we should be reduced to a set of pointings. In such a case, we could say nothing; we could only point. . . . Pure demonstration is a limit of approximation' (Stebbing, 1933d: 342; see also Janssen-Lauret, 2017: 14–15).[1]

Stebbing also expressed original views on what the distinctive characteristics of logic are, tracing out a line stretching from Aristotle to twentieth-century symbolic logic which stresses formality. Although

---

[1] See Janssen-Lauret (in press-c) for a case that Stebbing's argument here resembles that of Constance Jones and may have been influenced by Jones; see also Janssen-Lauret (2017) for a case that she may also have been influenced by Bradley.

Beaney and Chapman (2021: §2) state that Stebbing's book covers 'traditional, Aristotelian logic', Stebbing herself sharply distinguished between Aristotle's logic and that of those she called 'Traditional Logicians', certainly including the idealists Bosanquet and Bradley. Among Stebbing's original views on logic is the doctrine that Aristotle's logic shares with the symbolic logic of Frege, Peano, Russell, and Whitehead, but not with the thought of traditional logicians, a focus on formality. Early modern logicians and their successors argued over whether logic was an art, the 'art of thinking' – as in the title of the 1662 Port Royal Logic, *La logique ou l'art de penser* (Stebbing, 1930: 163) – or a science, and whether logic was psychologistic, that is, descriptive of reasoning, or normative, prescribing to us how we ought to think and argue. Stebbing's college principal Jones caused much controversy with her bold, anti-psychologistic stance that logic was the science of the relations between propositions (Jones, 1890).

Mathematical logic, which Stebbing called 'symbolic logic', cast new light on the question of the distinctive characteristics and subject matter of logic, the question now generally called 'logicality'. Previously, logicians and mathematicians had been content to build their systems up from principles which appeared to them to be intuitively true, or self-evident. But late nineteenth-century mathematicians had begun to find that coherent proof systems remained when some allegedly self-evident principles were given up. Non-Euclidean geometries, for example, no longer assumed that parallel lines never meet. Dedekind's definition of an infinite set assumes that such a set has a proper part which has the same (infinite) size as it, contradicting the intuitive principle that wholes are larger than their proper parts. And these kinds of unintuitive systems were soon given useful application in the new Einsteinian physics. Stebbing saw the importance of both the tendency of the new mathematical logic to rely increasingly on proof-theoretic methods and its applications to non-mathematical reality. She brought the two together in her philosophy of logic. Stebbing rejected Wittgenstein's view that logical truths do not say anything (Wittgenstein, 1922: 4.0312) because they are tautologous. She wrote, 'I think that the assertion of a tautology is a significant assertion . . . Further, I think that it is not absurd to say that a tautology is *true*' (Stebbing, 1933c: 196).

Stebbing held that the success of modern symbolic logic, which places no reliance on intuitive self-evidence, gives us good reason to dispense with self-evidence as a condition of logicality. It also places limits on the role played by modal notions in logic: 'We cannot answer that an axiom is a proposition that is necessarily true, for we do not know what *necessarily true* means' (Stebbing, 1930: 175). According to Stebbing, what is necessarily true is at best a relative notion given in terms of what is implied by what (Stebbing, 1930: 176). She also argued that we cannot rely on the notion of 'logical priority'. To speak of one truth being 'logically prior' to another is obscure and adds an inappropriate dose of metaphysics to our logic (Stebbing, 1930: 175). Stebbing concluded that 'no deductive system can be regarded as demonstrating necessarily true propositions by means of necessary primitive propositions or axioms' (Stebbing, 1930: 176–7) because truth cannot be established by proof in the sense of demonstration; to find out what is true we must turn to the empirical. What we can do is, in a given system, to take certain notions as undefined, and some statements as not for present purposes standing in need of proof, without their being taken to be absolutely indefinable or indemonstrable. These are called 'primitives' after Peano (Stebbing, 1930: 175). But what is the property that makes a system logic? Stebbing's answer was 'formality', not in the sense of involving only proof without invoking truth but in the sense of universal applicability.

> If we reject the view that there are different *logics*, then I think we can speak of logical principles which are exemplified in *every* deductive system and in every valid reasoning from premises to conclusion. It is the distinguishing characteristic of a logical principle that it applies not only to systems but to arguments, not only to geometries but to matters of fact. In other words, logical principles, are completely general because they are completely formal, and conversely. (Stebbing, 1933c: 196)

On Stebbing's view, then, logic is a science: the science which concerns what follows from what. The question of the nature of logical consequence, or what it means to say that something logically follows from something else, is also one on which Stebbing expressed original views. Stebbing discussed different kinds of logical following-from, first describing Russell's 'material implication', according to which *p* implies

q just in case either p is false or q is true (Stebbing, 1930: 223). She queried Russell's view that material implication is a plausible candidate for logical consequence. She cast doubt on that view by arguing that in ordinary language we say that, if q follows from p, then q can be deduced from p. Material implication, Stebbing countered, can hold between statements which cannot be deduced from one another. She expressed a preference for an alternative account of logical consequence, based on a relation which C. I. Lewis called 'strict implication' and Moore called 'entailment' (Stebbing, 1930: 222; see also Douglas & Nassim, 2021). The relation of entailment holds, for example, between statements like 'this is red' and 'this is coloured', that is, it covers what is now often called 'material consequence'. Entailment is not definable in psychological terms (Stebbing, 1930: 223). Although we would now categorise this kind of entailment as modal, Stebbing, in 1930, resisted this characterisation, arguing that 'impossible' is less clear than 'entails' (Stebbing, 1930: 222 n.1). Both implication and entailment are in turn distinct from inference, which Stebbing described as 'a mental process' (Stebbing, 1930: 210), and, although of interest to logic, different from validity. Inference is psychological, but not validity (Stebbing, 1930: 211).

These views of Stebbing's in turn affected her answers to the questions of extensionalism in logic and the relationship of logic to philosophy of science. The new mathematical logic's need to overcome intuition as a guide to logical truth, and replace it as far as possible with rules of proof, led to the rise of extensionalism. The extensionalist contends that we should talk about things as they are, not about how they may or must be. 'Mays' and 'musts', modal expressions, extensionalists took to rely on intuitions or psychological principles of self-evidence, methods made obsolete by the new mathematical logic. As we have seen, *Principia*'s aim was to speak of objects with referentially transparency, so that any two co-referential expressions were everywhere intersubstitutable (Whitehead & Russell, 1964 [1910]: appendix C). The radical extensionalist logicians of the 1930s and 1940s, especially Tarski and Quine, thought logic should only account for differences in extension, not intension: as Tarski put it, 'two concepts with different intensions but identical extensions are logically indistinguishable'

(Tarski, 1956 [1935]: 387). Quine, too, enthusiastically defended extensionalism (Quine, 2018 [1944]: 158; see also Janssen-Lauret, 2018, 2022b), and it was assumed that modal logics like C. I. Lewis's couldn't be extended to the quantified case until Ruth Barcan managed it in 1946–7 (Barcan, 1946, 1947).

We have seen that Stebbing was circumspect about allowing modality into logic. Yet she was not as strongly opposed to intensional discourse as Quine or Tarski. Stebbing certainly had reservations about ascribing necessity, especially essence or metaphysical necessity, to the world: 'Modern theories of organic evolution have combined with modern theories of mathematics to destroy the basis of the Aristotelian conception of essence' (Stebbing, 1930: 433). But she accepted analytic truth and admitted in a later paper that, although analyticity does not exhaust entailment, analytic containment 'involves a *must* which is a must of *necessity*' (Stebbing, 1933c: 193). Stebbing also expressed moderate extensionalism in her attitude towards intensions. She objected to the view that 'the intension of a word is commonly said to be all that we intend to mean by it' that 'this definition suggests an unfortunate intrusion of psychology into logic' (Stebbing, 1930: 28). But Stebbing, like Frege, believed that some intensional language could be systematised and decoupled from the psychological via quantification over abstract objects. Frege thought reference was made to senses where intersubstitutivity *salva veritate* failed (Frege, 1892). Stebbing did not believe in Fregean senses but nevertheless thought a set might have an intension as well as an extension, if the intension was taken to be its defining property (Stebbing, 1930: 141).

Stebbing's view of logic was in the main anti-psychologistic. She regarded logic as a science of what follows from what rather than one which describes how we in fact think. The anti-psychologistic view was typical of the grandparents and founders of analytic philosophy. Frege famously criticised psychologism in logic and mathematics. Jones, too, defended a view of logic as the normative science of how we ought to reason, given what the consequence relations between propositions are, rather than the descriptive science of reasoning, a branch of psychology (Jones, 1890: 2). Stebbing agreed with the view that logic is normative rather than a descriptive science of reasoning. But, according to her, the normativity of logic is simply a by-product of its abstract nature and its formality. Logic has no distinctive set of facts of its own; it traces the general forms of reality (Stebbing, 1930: 474). Nevertheless, Stebbing never lost sight of logic's connection to thinking and reasoning. She consistently described thinking as an activity. Logical reasoning she described as goal-directed, purposive thinking, separate not from action-linked thinking but from free association of thoughts or idle reverie. When giving examples of reasoning, she liked to give practical examples: a man uses his knowledge of natural laws to trace a safe path off a cliff in high tide (Stebbing, 1930: 1–2); a woman thinks through why it is unwise to wear a given dress to the beach, as the chemically unstable dye fades in sea air (Stebbing, 1930: 8); a man locked out of his flat devises hypotheses which he can test in order to determine whether the flat has been burgled (Stebbing, 1930: 234). Stebbing viewed logical reasoning as an activity of people, people who interact in communities and whose views are informed by the 'intellectual climate' (Stebbing, 1930: 294) in which they live.

Lastly, a central aspect of Stebbing's outlook was her view of logic as continuous with philosophy of science and scientific methodology. Stebbing did not favour a split of logic into an inductive and a deductive branch, since she believed that science must deploy both inductive and deductive reasoning (Stebbing, 1930: 245, 344). What is true in a natural science, unlike in a purely deductive science such as mathematics, 'depends upon what there actually is in the world' (Stebbing, 1930: 231) and relies on experience (Stebbing, 1930: 232). But scientific method stands in continuity with logic because the task of the natural sciences is to construct a system of the world. Stebbing carefully reflected on the nature of a system. In a certain sense, any collection of elements standing in relations is a system (Stebbing, 1930: 174). Deductive systems specifically are composed of propositions – defined by her as something a thinker or speaker can affirm or deny (Stebbing, 1930: 15) – standing in logical relations. But Stebbing also spoke of systems as composed of facts, with the requirement that the facts all be mutually consistent with each other; she speaks of facts as contradictory 'when the propositions which would correspond to those facts are contradictory' (Stebbing, 1930: 199). Following the revolution in rigour and the great success and applicability of unintuitive proof systems like transfinite arithmetic and non-Euclidean geometry, we can no longer assume that systems rest on self-evident axioms or are false when they have counter-intuitive consequences. Nor can we assume that the world itself is a system. It is certainly not logically necessary that it is. Yet science, Stebbing wrote, is concerned with finding '*the* system (if there is one) which is *the system of the world*' (Stebbing, 1930: 199).

Since logic, according to Stebbing, is formal in a sense where it is concerned with truth, the label of 'logic' can be usefully applied to the kind of method which seeks increasingly abstract generalisations which take observations as a point of departure: we begin with awareness of a complex situation in which some fact is singled out as peculiar, to be accounted for, we form a hypothesis connecting it to other facts, and develop the hypothesis deductively, in order to test the consequences so deduces against observable facts (Stebbing, 1930: 234–5). We might now call Stebbing's procedure here a version of the hypothetico-deductive method. Stebbing did not view the hypothetico-deductive method and the inductive method as opposed. In her view, both are involved in scientific reasoning. She viewed inductive reasoning as resulting not from mere enumeration of cases (this crow is black, that crow is black, ..., therefore all crows are black) but from a combination of enumeration and analogy. Inductive reasoning consists not just of enumeration but also of finding respects of resemblance, shared properties of scientific relevance, between the instances: we can call a bird a 'crow' only if it resembles 'in certain respects other others called by the same name ... properties belonging to all the instances of crows constitute the total positive analogy' (Stebbing, 1930: 250). Stebbing considered argument by metaphor in the scientific context especially pernicious because she regarded a metaphor as an especially weak analogy, connoting only one shared property (Stebbing, 1930: 253). What sort of a system is a scientific theory? Stebbing was sympathetic to the then fashionable view that science does not explain (that is, it does not answer why-questions) but instead describes; it answers how-questions. Yet she pointed out that science does not merely describe in the sense of listing propositions which recount all the scientific facts, such as exact descriptions of which motions occurred or which particles were present in which location at which time. Such descriptions are neither feasible nor useful.

Scientific theorising requires abstraction and formulations of law-like generalisations: 'constructive description', in Stebbing's terminology (Stebbing, 1930: 392).

The facts which comprise the world include those which resist systematisation without first being subjected to some abstraction in thought. When we perceive, we perceive absolutely specific shades and sounds, for which we have no words. To use words is already to abstract to some degree. To use general terms is to classify (Stebbing, 1930: 444). The most abstract propositions are formal ones. Their significance is independent of any specific experience (Stebbing, 1930: 446). How, asked Stebbing, can we link the neat, orderly, exact system of science to the 'untidy, fragmentary world of common sense' to which our absolutely specific, unstructured perceptions belong? We use not merely the abstractions which naming, classifying, hypothesising, and law-like generalising afford us but also the method of extensive abstraction due to Whitehead. Stebbing's example is Whitehead's account of points. First, we take the relation of spatial inclusion, as when a box fits inside another box. We define inclusion as a transitive, asymmetric, serial relation and say that a point is what that series of inclusion converges on. We need not know anything about the intrinsic nature of points. All we need is their formal properties (Stebbing, 1930: 451). Points, then, are logical constructions, but they are not fictions. They are constructed not in the sense of being made up but in the sense of discovery (Stebbing, 1930: 454). They help us theorise.

Stebbing's contributions to logic are deserving of wider recognition among historians of analytic philosophy. Her *Modern Introduction to Logic* was the first accessible book on symbolic logic and also contained innovative material on a range of topics in the philosophy of logic. Stebbing carefully considered what formality, the hallmark of logic, means in view of new developments in proof theory which imply that logic can no longer lay claim to being self-evident or necessarily true. Stebbing gave an original and sophisticated answer, namely one in terms of the universal applicability of logic. She also made progress on the topics of analysis and incomplete symbol theory. She distinguished analytic analyses, such as mathematical definitions, from philosophical analyses, briefly sketching an account of philosophical analysis that is not analytic, and thereby laid the groundwork for her later metaphysics, and made room for a more holist approach within analytic philosophy.

3 Philosophy of Science

Much of Susan Stebbing's published work focussed on the philosophy of science and especially on the philosophy of physics. But it is only very recently that she has been given credit for holding original views on philosophy of science (West, 2022; Janssen-Lauret, 2022a). To date, little has been written about the half-dozen philosophy of science papers Stebbing published between 1924 and 1929, where she set out her view, which she termed 'realism', on the importance of observations to philosophy of science (Stebbing, 1924, 1924–5, 1926, 1927, 1928, 1929). As we saw in Section 2.1, Stebbing's *Modern Introduction to Logic* had much to say on the relationship between logic and scientific methodology. Yet, to date, it has not seen much engagement from historians of analytic philosophy. Her book *Philosophy and the Physicists* (Stebbing, 1937) investigated and meticulously rebutted the idealistic interpretation of Einsteinian physics and quantum mechanics then popular with some physicists. Stebbing's contemporaries described the book as having a wholly negative project (Broad, 1938; Paul, 1938). But current scholarship has begun to argue that Stebbing put her original ideas to good use in *Philosophy and the Physicists*, such as directional analysis (Janssen-Lauret, 2022a; see also Section 4 in this Element) as well as novel views on entropy (West, 2022). Stebbing continued to write on philosophy of physics until the final years of her life (Stebbing, 1942–3).

If it appears surprising that little attention has been paid to Stebbing's philosophy of science and physics, this may be connected to the perception that Stebbing was primary a follower of Moore. Moore, captivated from a young age by the question of idealism, represented in its various branches by Kant and Bradley, never studied much physics and had little to say on its philosophy. In her philosophy of physics, Stebbing mentioned Moore only rarely. In her early papers, she entered into a dialogue mainly with the philosopher of physics and logician A. N. Whitehead. She also engaged in symposia with other philosophers of physics such as C. D. Broad, Dorothy Wrinch, and R. B. Braithwaite. In *Philosophy and the Physicists*, Stebbing never mentioned Moore. She focussed primarily on her critique of the idealist physicist Arthur Eddington, also engaging along the way with other analytic philosophers such as Bertrand Russell, C. D. Broad, and C. E. M. Joad, and other idealist physicists like James Jeans. The views on perception and observation which Stebbing developed in the 1920s do not much resemble Moore's, and her extended and sophisticated arguments for anti-idealism about physics are, I argue, best interpreted as distinct from Moorean common-sense philosophy. A closer look at Stebbing's philosophy of physics furthers the case that she deserves to be known as an important analytic philosopher in her own right.

Stebbing's achievements appear even more impressive given that she was almost entirely self-educated in physics. As we saw in Section 1, she had been only intermittently homeschooled as a Victorian girl with a disability. Although interested in studying natural science (Chapman, 2013: 11), Stebbing was unable to make this wish a reality as an undergraduate student because she was left disabled by Ménière's disease. Its attendant attacks of vertigo, dizziness, and nausea made it in practice impossible for Stebbing to work in a laboratory. Still, she never lost her interest in physics. So it should not come as a surprise that Stebbing's first venture into analytic philosophy concerned the interpretation of the new Einsteinian physics.

Here, Stebbing made an early move to spur on the development of analytic philosophy from a heavily foundationalist project to one adaptable to the holism that was distinctive of mid-analytic philosophy.

3.1 Stebbing's Early Papers: Whiteheadian Philosophy of Science, Observations, and Realism

While historians often present the origins of analytic philosophy as lying entirely with the early efforts of Russell and Moore, and thus as sparked primarily by anti-idealism, in my view an important driving force for the development of analytic philosophy was the pressure to find a philosophy to make sense of the new science and mathematics and their counter-intuitive consequences. Stebbing's philosophy of physics was both anti-idealist and concerned to account for novel developments in mathematics and science. In Section 2.1, we saw her carefully considering the repercussions for logic of the new science and mathematics, which imply that we can no longer assume that it is necessarily true that parallel lines never meet, or that wholes are always greater in size than their proper parts, simply because they seem intuitively self-evident. It was not merely that assuming the falsity of such apparently intuitive principles led to perfectly coherent proof systems. Such proof systems, of non-Euclidean geometry and set theories which allowed for denumerable and non-denumerable infinities, were also fruitfully applied to model the space–time of Einstein's theory of general relativity. So, what had appeared to be self-evident necessary truths about parallel lines never meeting and wholes always being greater than their proper parts now seemed to be actual falsehoods, not true of the physical world in their complete generality. Stebbing saw the need for a properly worked-out philosophy to fit around the deliverances of the new natural sciences. In her work on logic, as we have seen, she argued that we may explain 'how the exact and tidy world of the physicist is connected with the fragmentary and untidy world of common sense [if we] demonstrate the applicability of abstract deductive systems to the world given in sense-experience' (Stebbing, 1930: 452) and that we should turn to Whiteheadian extensive abstraction to carry out this project.

As we saw in Section 1, the prevailing narrative of Stebbing's development has it that she was 'converted' to Moorean analytic philosophy as a result of a philosophical exchange with Moore in 1917–18 (e.g. Beaney & Chapman, 2021: §3). Although Stebbing herself was to an extent responsible for this 'conversion' account (Stebbing, 1942: 530), it must be borne in mind that the paper in which she made this claim was explicitly a homage to Moore, written in Stebbing's final years while she was very unwell, and with a generally self-abnegatory tone throughout, and that Stebbing was apt to be overly modest at the best of times (Janssen-Lauret, 2022a; Connell & Janssen-Lauret, in press: §1). It is true that Stebbing certainly did turn away from idealism and towards analytic philosophy. Still, her publications during the 1920s were not Moorean in focus. They engaged in dialogue primarily with Whitehead's philosophy of physics and at times expressed explicit disagreement with Moore.

Whiteheadian philosophy of physics is vast, complex, and written in a language of its own full of neologisms. Space does not permit me to give a full account of his thought here, although I will highlight a few key parts (see MacBride, 2018: 115–28, for a fuller treatment). Whitehead thought that for a realist philosophy to encompass Einsteinian physics required some radical shifts in our thinking. Among these shifts was a symbolic logic to replace the Aristotelian subject-predicate model, in order to represent the relational and polyadic (multiple-quantifier) logical forms of relational statements, such as those used in his account of spatial points: in between any two points, there is another point, and neither the points nor their names can be listed. We must give up the binary opposition of subject-predicate form in logic and the grammar of our language. More than this, Whitehead thought, to grasp the new physics fully we must also dispense with the distinction between particular and universal, which results 'from our inveterate habit of forcing all philosophies into the framework of Aristotelian categories; and finally, from an undue reliance upon the ultimate philosophical importance of Indo-European languages' (Stebbing, 1924–5: 313). It was not just the two-category treatment of particular and universal which Whitehead deplored but the 'Bifurcation of Nature' more generally. Nature does not divide into the neat binaries we were taught by previous generations of philosophers. We must also do away with the distinctions between mind and body and primary and secondary quality. Rather, Nature must be thought of as an endless succession of events, from which both common-sense objects – plants, animals, persons, rocks, planets – and their qualities and relations are abstractions. There is no ultimate sense to be made of a distinction between the primary qualities an object really has, such as its size, shape, and motion, and the secondary qualities which are mental additions, such as colour, sound, and smell. All these qualities are to be found in Nature. All are to an extent abstractions from the panoply of events which it comprises, as is the mind itself (Stebbing, 1924: 292).

Stebbing agreed that the Bifurcation of Nature must be abandoned, but took a more moderate view than Whitehead. From early on, she expressed a preference for an ontology of particulars and universals – though one which included relational universals, not merely properties – which together combine into facts, instead of Whitehead's event ontology. Yet she admitted that the nature of the particular-universal distinction was far from obvious and must be carefully revisited in view of the difficulties with its application to physics. She explicitly took issue with Moore's common-sense derivation of the particular-universal distinction from the distinction between what is predicable and what is not: 'Prof. Moore says "is predicable of something else" is a perfectly clear notion . . . I am rather doubtful' (Stebbing, 1924–5: 316). By contrast, Stebbing came to embrace the Whiteheadian view that secondary qualities are really there in Nature. They are not an addition made by our minds. She further cautioned against the extrusion of mind from nature, including, as we shall see, in *Philosophy and the Physicists*. Her arguments for these positions, though, often differed from Whitehead's. She put forward original views about the basis of ordinary-language observational truths needed by physics and philosophy alike.

Stebbing held that there is a certain kind of collection of facts such that they 'can all be known, and that such facts are the basis upon which all scientific and philosophical speculation must rest' (Stebbing, 1929: 147). But these were quite different in kind from the propositions Moore offered up to the reader as certain, such as 'Hens lay eggs' (Stebbing, 1933b: 8). Stebbing's basis for scientific and philosophical speculation was what she called 'perceptual science' (Stebbing, 1929: 148), comprising statements such as:

1. I am now seeing a red patch.
2. I am now perceiving a piece of blotting paper.
3. That is a piece of blotting paper.
4. That piece of blotting paper is on the table.
5. That piece of blotting paper was on the table before I saw it.
6. Other people besides myself have seen that piece of blotting paper.
   (Stebbing, 1929: 147)

The view that (1)–(6) above are true and known to be true Stebbing called 'realism'. Her 'realism' was clearly distinct from Moore's 'Common-Sense View', often described as one according to which 'our ordinary common-sense view of the world is largely correct' (Baldwin, 2004: §6), even though there are some similarities. Stebbing's range of truths was narrower, and more perception-focussed, than Moore's. Stebbing also emphasised that she saw both philosophy and physics as starting from the same range of truths about perceptual observations, the relationship of the observer to her perceptions, and her relationship to other observing subjects. By contrast, Moore never mentioned physics when enumerating certainties or truisms. Stebbing contended that 'the denial of realism is inconsistent with the validity of physical theories... theoretical physics has developed by the continual modification of common-sense views through a stage of what might be called perceptual science, and that unless perceptual science is true theoretical physics cannot be true' (Stebbing, 1929: 148). Stebbing's 'perceptual science', or 'realism', is commonsensical in a certain way but much more naturalistic than Moore's 'Common-Sense View'.

Crucially, Stebbing did not take her 'realism' to entail the falsity of most forms of idealism. Her realism does plausibly entail the falsity of Bradley's realism specifically. After all, Bradley held the idiosyncratic view that Reality, being fundamentally one and without structure, could never in principle be truly described by ordinary human language. But Stebbing held that most ontologically idealist theories are not like Bradley's. They do not say that (1)–(6) are false but rather that there is a philosophical analysis according to which the objects discussed in (1)–(6) have a mental or spiritual, rather than material, nature. Stebbing wrote, 'does physics give us any reason to suppose that propositions such as the six propositions I asserted above are false? I cannot see that it does... It has relevance to naive realism, which is a theory about the analysis of such propositions' (Stebbing, 1929: 147). Naïve realism provides a physicalist analysis of (1)–(6). Moore also placed weight on the distinction between knowing a truth and knowing its analysis, and Stebbing cited his 1925 'Defence of Common Sense' here for that insight. Nevertheless, Stebbing's view had already moved beyond Moore's at this point. According to Stebbing, modern physical theory was in tension with naïve realism, but not with her realism, and by itself neither compelled nor ruled out an idealist interpretation of physics.

3.2 Stebbing's *Philosophy and the Physicists*

Stebbing's 1937 book *Philosophy and the Physicists* presented an extended argument against idealist interpretations of modern physics, largely those of the physicist Arthur Eddington and to a lesser extent James Jeans, also a physicist. As Stebbing made no positive case in favour of an alternative interpretation of modern physics, her contemporaries took her project to be wholly negative, merely cleaning up the mess made by physicists going beyond their competence and wandering into the realm of philosophy. Broad's (otherwise complimentary) review made a rather sexist comparison between Stebbing and 'a good housewife who has at least completed her spring-cleaning' (Broad, 1938: 226). But the fact that Stebbing's case was largely critical, and she presented no alternative interpretation of physics, does not imply that her arguments were merely of the nature of picking apart (and sweeping up) Eddington's and Jeans's arguments.

Recent commentators have argued that Stebbing drew upon her original philosophical thought in the course of *Philosophy and the Physicists*, even though she did not always make clear when she did this. West (2022) argues that Stebbing defended an original view on the philosophy of entropy (Stebbing, 1937: chap. 11). I will show here that Stebbing also argued for her Whitehead-inspired view that secondary qualities are in Nature (Stebbing, 1937: 52–5), appealed to her 1930 proposal that science provides a 'constructive description' (Stebbing, 1937: 85), and used her views on philosophical analysis and logical constructions to further her argumentative case. Idealists about physics, on Stebbing's view, believe that successive steps of analysis ultimately reveal physical objects to be logical constructions out of something mental, 'the stuff of our consciousness' (Eddington, 1920: 200). Stebbing was not dogmatically opposed to idealist interpretations of physics. She even called some of Eddington's statements of idealism 'delightful' (Stebbing, 1937: 208). But whether an idealist interpretation of physics is viable must depend on the merits of the philosophical analysis it provides and the arguments offered in favour of it. Stebbing judged Eddington's arguments to be insufficient to establish idealism.[2] What follows is not a full account of all of Eddington's arguments or Stebbing's rebuttals; due to constraints of space, I have to restrict my discussion to a few highlights.

It is important to make clear at the outset that Stebbing did not take the statement that physical objects are logical constructions out of elements which are ultimately mental or spiritual in nature to be in any way internally contradictory. Stebbing's position was that modern theories of

---

[2] Eddington's view is now often called 'panpsychism', but Stebbing did not use that term.

physics entailed neither idealism nor materialism. To suppose otherwise was, Stebbing thought, to commit the fallacy of supposing that a macro-object – that is, a logical construction, really a plurality of micro-objects in some arrangement – inherits the properties of the micro-objects which make it up, or vice versa. We saw in Section 2.1 that in her work on logical constructions, Stebbing compared this fallacy to 'the confusion in supposing that if *men are numerous* and *Socrates is a man*, it would follow that *Socrates is numerous*' (Stebbing, 1933a: 505).

Materialists as well as idealists may fall into the above fallacy. Nineteenth-century materialist physicists did so, Stebbing noted, when, having discovered the atom, they assumed that atoms were 'solid, absolutely hard, indivisible billiard-ball-like . . . in a perfectly straight-forward sense of the words "solid" and "hard" ' (Stebbing, 1937: 47). When Rutherford split the atom, physicists came to know that atoms were not, in fact, solid, but consisted of subatomic particles suspended in mostly empty space. But Eddington, too, committed a version of the fallacy which conflates the properties of the macro-objects with those of their constituent micro-objects. He did so, for example, when inferring from the fact that the atoms of which a plank in his study floor is made are mostly empty space that 'the plank has no solidity' (Eddington, 1928: 342). To say 'the plank is not solid' in ordinary English is to imply that the plank is very brittle or visibly has holes in it. Stebbing maintained that it remains, despite our knowledge of subatomic particles, perfectly true to say 'this plank is solid' of an ordinarily robust plank free of worrisome holes. That the plank is, at the subatomic level, made up of mostly empty space is perhaps counter-intuitive but does not negate its solidity. 'No concepts drawn from the level of common-sense thinking are appropriate to sub-atomic, i.e. microphysical, phenomena' (Stebbing, 1937: 44). The macro-object, a plank, which we generally describe in ordinary language, is solid; the micro-objects, atoms, which comprise its analysis, are not themselves solid; these two statements are not mutually contradictory.

Similarly, the macro-objects are called 'material objects' in ordinary language, but there is no contradiction in supposing that their micro-components might, as Eddington supposed, be made of 'the stuff of consciousness'. It may appear that a follower of Moore's 'Common-Sense View' ought to find such a view contradictory. We will see in Section 4 that Moore at times seemed to incline towards the position that such a view is paradoxical. Stebbing, by contrast, did not. She was very clear that Eddington's purported analysis, 'the plank is material but its ultimate micro-constituents are the stuff of consciousness', is no more internally contradictory than 'the plank is solid but its component atoms are mostly empty space'. Stebbing's objection to Eddington's idealist conclusion was not that it was internally contradictory or at odds with common sense. She simply found that it did not follow from his premises.

By Stebbing's lights, Eddington's project went wrong early on not just by committing the fallacy of conflating macro-objects' properties with those of their constituents but by raising the question 'how is perception possible?', a question which Stebbing (for Whiteheadian reasons) already considered 'devoid of sense' (Stebbing, 1937: 52), and by looking to physics for an answer to it. Stebbing, of course, held that physics itself must rest on facts about perception and observation, and relationships between observers, and although she did not cite her 1929 account of 'perceptual science' in *Philosophy and the Physicists* I will show that she made use of it. What's more, Stebbing objected to the Bifurcation of Nature inherent in Eddington's view that physics constructs a 'symbolic world'. Eddington's 'symbolic world' duplicates the familiar world in which, for example, Susan Stebbing stepped into her study and took pleasure in seeing and smelling 'a crimson and scented rose' from a bowl on her desk. On Eddington's account, the world of physics contains 'duplicates' of the desk, the bowl, the rose, etcetera. It contains no duplicate of crimson but merely 'its scientific equivalent electromagnetic wavelength...the wave is the reality...the colour is mere mind-spinning' (Eddington, 1928: 88). Stebbing felt that Eddington was correct to deny that the wave itself is coloured, for we must not 'in one and the same sentence...mix up language used appropriately for the furniture of earth and our daily dealings with it with language used for the purpose of philosophical and scientific discussion' (Stebbing, 1937: 42).[3] Nevertheless, the wave not being coloured cannot be used as a premise to support the conclusion that the *rose* is not really coloured

---

[3] See Chapman (2013) for an interpretation of *Philosophy and the Physicists* which emphasises the difference between ordinary language and the language of physics.

(Stebbing, 1937: 51). The rose, a macro-object, is instead to be analysed in terms which include the electromagnetic wavelength.

The distinction between primary qualities – such as length, breadth, mass, shape, and motion – which physical objects really have, and secondary qualities assumed to be mental additions – such as colour, sound, and smell – was one Whitehead and Stebbing deplored. The distinction had nevertheless been common among philosophers since the seventeenth century. Stebbing cited examples from Newton, affirming the distinction, and from Berkeley, criticising Locke and the Cartesians for holding it (Stebbing, 1937: 51–5). Eddington went further than Newton, Locke, and the Cartesians had done. In his 'scientific world', he found not just equivalents of secondary qualities but duplicates of their subjects, too. He claimed to be writing his book sitting at two tables at once.

> Two tables! Yes, there are duplicates of every object about me ... One of them has been familiar to me from earliest years ... it has extension, it is comparatively permanent; it is coloured; above all, it is substantial ... Table No. 2 is my scientific table ... There is nothing substantial about my second table. It is nearly all empty space. (Eddington, 1928: xi–xii)

In isolation, the above might seem like a harmless metaphorical use of language. But Eddington emphasised that he meant the language of duplicates of each object existing in 'a spiritual world alongside the physical world' (Eddington, 1928: 288) literally. On Stebbing's view, the positing of two tables alongside each other was simply a mistake. The familiar table is a logical construct. We all understand, at the level of ordinary language, what it means to say that it is solid, coloured, and substantial. The atoms which are mostly empty space and the fields which oscillate to produce electromagnetic waves are resultants of analysis. They reside at the level of the most basic facts of physics. These basic facts are composed of elements which, as far as we know, are simple. What can correctly be predicated of them cannot be predicated of the table. At least, we cannot make such predications without careful qualification; we may be able to say, 'at the subatomic level, the table consists mostly of empty space'. This statement sounds counter-intuitive but may constitute a summary of an appropriate, physical analysis of the ordinary, solid table. The new mathematics taught us that we cannot deny that infinite sets have proper parts the same size as them just because it sounds counter-intuitive. The same is true of the analysis of the table in terms of atoms which are themselves mostly empty space. Its counter-intuitive appearance is not grounds to declare it false. Nor does it give us reason to posit two tables, one solid and one tenuous.

Eddington's reduplications further forced a strong and, according to Stebbing, unhelpful Bifurcation of Nature into mind and body. She described the way Eddington compared the human mind to a newspaper office providing a 'free translation' of 'messages' from the outside world. These messages we, or rather 'the editor' in our mind, that is, 'the perceiving part of our mind' (Stebbing, 1937: 84), 'dress' with colour, space, and substance which are not really there (Stebbing, 1937: 82). Stebbing objected that Eddington relied on the metaphor of the newspaper editor not as an illustration of something further to be explained but as an argument by analogy. Eddington offered up this argument in support of the conclusions that our belief in the external world is 'a remote inference' (Stebbing, 1937: 85), that we know the world only because 'its fibres stretch into our consciousness', and that yet we have grounds to identify it with what is in common between many consciousnesses (Stebbing, 1937: 87). We have seen in Section 2.1 that Stebbing generally deplored the use of metaphor as argument in philosophy of science because she categorised metaphors, in that context, as reasoning from weak analogy (Stebbing, 1930: 253–4). The 'editor' metaphor is no different; the analogy between the perceiving part of our mind and a newspaper editor soon breaks down. Stebbing, then, saw no reason to revise her views on the basis of Eddington's argument from analogy. She maintained her Whiteheadian view that the external world is not inferred from perceptions but directly apprehended: 'there is equally no doubt that we are able, as a result of our past experience, immediately to perceive that this is a so-and-so. In such immediate recognition no inference is involved' (Stebbing, 1930: 211). She reiterated the same conclusion for which she had found support in her 1929 'perceptual science' view that physics need not justify other minds because they are inevitably presupposed by its method: 'Physics as a science results from the conjoint labour of many minds or persons' (Stebbing, 1937: 108). Stebbing wondered whether Eddington's mention of 'fibres' of consciousness constituted a further metaphor and was inclined to think not (Stebbing, 1937: 85); Eddington derived the conclusion that we really only know our own consciousness and that nerve impulses do not resemble the external world 'in intrinsic nature' (Stebbing, 1937: 86).

Stebbing was sympathetic to part of Eddington's case, in particular to his suggestion that physics does not tell us the intrinsic nature of things. After all, physics abstracts away from the macro-individuals, with their absolutely determinate qualities which we are in touch with, in favour of a constructed system of generalities which details their relations to each other: their extrinsic connections. Stebbing wrote, '"the world of physics" is nothing but a constructed system stated in terms of imperceptibles, the system being such that it permits, under certain conditions, of interpretation by reference to perceptual elements' (Stebbing, 1933–4: 9). She could sympathise with some of Eddington's structuralist assumptions, familiar to her from Russell and Carnap (Stebbing 1934b), including the suggestion that the information physics gives us allows for multiple interpretations as long as those interpretations share the structure of the information provided: 'A constructed system may be capable of interpretation in terms of a given set of facts. It may then be adequate to this set, but it could never be exhaustive . . . physics is abstract' (Stebbing, 1933–4: 25).

Stebbing's view, dating back to her 1920s papers, that modern physics is in itself compatible with either an idealist or a materialist interpretation also provides support for the conclusion that physics does not reveal the intrinsic natures of things. She criticised the overconfidence of nineteenth-century materialist physicists who felt very sure that they knew the intrinsic nature of matter and atoms (Stebbing, 1937: 96). Yet Eddington (unlike Stebbing) assumed that there nevertheless is some intrinsic nature to be known and that we have reason to assume that it is conscious. He began by arguing that there are '(a) a mental image, which is in our minds and not in the external world; (b) some kind of counterpart in the external world, which is of inscrutable nature; (c) a set of pointer-readings, which exact science can study' (Eddington, 1928: 254). He then added the premises that the schedule of pointer-readers must be 'attached to some unknown background' and that 'for pointer-readers of my own brain I have an insight which is not limited to the evidence of pointer-readings. That insight shows that they are attached to a background of consciousness' (Eddington, 1928: 259). He concludes that 'it has a nature capable of manifesting itself as mental activity'. Stebbing was unimpressed, declaring the argument 'a complete muddle' (Stebbing, 1937: 99). Perhaps Eddington has insight into what is going on in his own consciousness, she countered, but he has no such self-knowledge about his brain, much less direct insight into the attachment of any pointer-readings concerning his brain to his consciousness. Knowledge about what the pointer-readers concerning one's own brain say is knowledge inferred from that of pointer-readers concerning other people's brains. There is no direct insight here.

How, then, are we to settle the question what physics is about? Stebbing believed that progress might be made by careful philosophical analysis, but this would always be a piecemeal project of assessing individual idealist or materialist proposals. Stebbing wrote,

> it seems to me quite clear that the new physics does not imply idealism. Neither, however, does it imply materialism . . . There are problems in plenty to be dealt with concerning the inter-connexions of mental and bodily activity, but none of these problems are in any way affected by developments in physics. To pursue this topic further it would be necessary to consider in detail the various abstractions by means of which we are able to divide 'the sciences' up, assigning some problems to physicists, some to chemists, some to biochemists, some to physiologists, and some to psychologists. (Stebbing, 1942–3, 184)

In her final works on the question, then, Stebbing appeared to suggest what we would now call a naturalistic line. She continued to believe that analytic philosophers ought to search for a philosophy which could fit around the latest results of the sciences and was now beginning to make explicit room for at least some social sciences within this project, given her mention of psychology. Psychology had begun to separate itself from 'mental philosophy' from the early analytic period and was beginning to grow into a quantitative science to be reckoned with. According to Stebbing, the question whether idealism, materialism, dualism, or some other alternative is true should be addressed by collaboration between practitioners of different sciences plus well-informed philosophers of science.

4 Metaphysics

Stebbing's metaphysics, especially her distinction between metaphysical and grammatical analysis, is the part of her oeuvre which has so far received the most attention from historians of analytic philosophy. Older texts which mention Stebbing (e.g. Urmson, 1956; Passmore, 1966) focus on her views on metaphysical analysis. Many recent commentators (Beaney, 2003; Milkov, 2003; Beaney, 2016) do the same but tend to describe her view repeatedly as 'Moorean' (see also Section 1).[4] Milkov even applies Moore's name to a position which Stebbing claimed as her own, giving the name 'Moore's directional analysis' (Milkov, 2003: 358) to what Stebbing herself describes (in a paper about Moore) as 'an analysis I once called "directional analysis" '(Stebbing, 1942: 527). Of course, Stebbing acknowledged a debt to Moore in her work on analysis. But, in my view, it can be shown that Stebbing's directional analysis in fact made a key advance on Moore. She succeeded in solving at least one key problem which baffled Moore in his 'Defence of Common Sense', as we will see in this section. Stebbing made interesting contributions to several other areas of metaphysics, too, such as the metaphysics of language, causation, and mereology. But due to limitations of space, I will discuss the former only in passing and hope to cover the latter two in future work.

Stebbing's distinction between metaphysical and grammatical analysis constituted progress in philosophy. In effect, we may think of her distinction and the use she put it to as having already solved the paradox of analysis ten years before Langford formulated it (Langford, 1942). Langford presented the paradox as a conundrum for Moore's views on analysis, in the form of a dilemma. Do the common-sense propositions which Moore calls 'truisms' (Moore, 1925: 32) and their analyses have the same meaning? If the answer is 'yes', then the analysis conveys no more than the original truism; then analysis is pointless and trivial. But if the answer is 'no', the two do not have the same meaning; then the analysis is false. Langford wrote, 'One is tempted to say that there must be some appropriate sense of 'meaning' in which the two verbal expressions

---

[4] Coliva (2021) is an exception.

do have the same meaning and some other appropriate sense in which they do not' (Langford, 1942: 323).

Stebbing had provided an explication of these two different senses of 'meaning' in 1932. Unlike Moore, Stebbing had, from at least 1930, insisted that the philosopher analyses not propositions but sentences or sub-sentential expressions (Stebbing, 1930: 155, 441). She also clarified that definitions do not define objects, or concepts, but expressions (Stebbing, 1930: 439–41). Two years later, she made use of this view to dispel the conflation between different kinds of 'meaning' which Langford would complain about ten years afterwards. Stebbing wrote, 'For my purpose it is sufficient to consider only two kinds of intellectual analysis, namely, grammatical analysis and metaphysical analysis. In grammatical analysis the elements of a sentence, viz., words, are detected. . . . Grammatical analysis is analysis at what might be called the same level' (Stebbing, 1932–33: 77–8). She then sharply distinguished grammatical analysis from metaphysical analysis: 'The metaphysician is concerned with what the words refer to, i.e., with the constituents there must be in the world if the sentence is so used as to say what is true' (Stebbing, 1932–33: 78).

Grammatical, or same-level, analysis explains a sentence in terms of another stretch of language. Such analysis, if it consists in definition, or conceptual analysis, may well be a priori, or analytically true. By contrast, metaphysical analyses are never analytic or a priori. Metaphysical analysis describes what facts, with which components, the world will contain in case the sentence is true. We should not expect to know this a priori. Nor should we expect always to be able to recognise, without inspecting the world, whether a sentence and its metaphysical analysis are synonymous. Which individuals, in which configurations, the world contains is an a posteriori matter; to know it, we have to inspect the world: 'metaphysical analysis presupposes certain assumptions with regard to the constitution of the world. These assumptions are not logically necessary' (Stebbing, 1932–33: 80). The paradox of analysis is solved by separating grammatical analysis, where sameness of linguistic meaning is often expected, from directional analysis, which searches for the reference, not the discursive meaning, of a sentence.

In 1932, Stebbing wrote about directional analysis as to an extent inspired by Moore – though noting that she did not 'wish to suggest . . . that he would agree with what I say' (Stebbing, 1932–3: 76). By contrast, a few months later, in 1933, she firmly cordoned off her own philosophical method from Moore's. She wrote, 'Where he, in his later and clearer statement, speaks of "understanding *the meaning of a proposition*" I prefer to speak of "understanding a *sentence*". Where he speaks of "knowing what a proposition *means* in the sense of being able *to give a correct analysis of its meaning*" I prefer to speak of 'knowing *the analysis of a sentence*", (Stebbing, 1933b: 9). Moore's difficulty in accounting for the two different kinds of 'meaning' required in analysis rested, Stebbing obliquely pointed out, on his failure to be maximally clear about what the objects of analysis are. To solve the conundrum over 'meaning', we must first focus on the analysis of sentences, not propositions.

Stebbing's distinction allows us to solve a problem which Moore raised in his published writings but was unable to dispense with. In his anti-idealist paper 'Defence of Common Sense', Moore started off strong but ended in a kind of aporia. Insisting that his common sense 'truisms', like 'There exists at present a living human body, which is my body' and 'The earth has existed for many years past', were known 'with certainty' (Moore, 1925: 32–3) ruled out relatively few versions of idealism. It was certainly incompatible with the idiosyncratic idealism of Bradley. Bradley, we have seen, did hold that ordinary-language truisms were not ultimately true because they misrepresented the structureless One-ness of Reality. But then, towards the end of his paper, Moore tried to use philosophical analysis to rule out more conventional forms of ontological idealism. He found that he could not manage to do so.

An assumption which Stebbing took over from Moore was that, however certain we may be of a given truism, no specific analysis follows from it. Suppose I am convinced of the certain truth of 'This is a human hand', while looking at my hand. I cannot see all of my hand at once, so I must begin with sense-data, the things I can perceive directly. Moore attempted three analyses of 'This is a human hand', all of which fail. Each attempt at an analysis starts with 'This [sense-datum] is part of the surface of a human hand'. The first attempt lays out a totally materialist analysis, according to which hands are physical objects, logical constructions out of physical sense-data. Physical sense-data are just the surfaces of physical objects. This first analysis cannot account for double vision, so Moore dismissed it as inadequate for his purposes. The second analysis takes hands to be material, sense-data mental. Moore dismissed this analysis, too, because of its reliance on the mysterious relation of 'being an appearance of'. The last kind of analysis is idealist. Sense-data are mental and hands are logical constructions out of sense data. Moore could not see how to rule out this analysis or declare it categorically worse than the first and second alternatives, but it clearly gave him pause, as he called it 'paradoxical' (Moore, 1925: 59). His use of the word 'paradoxical' may suggest that he had some preliminary awareness of a version of the paradox of analysis. But I hypothesise that the paradox Moore had in mind here resulted from the contrast between common sense labelling hands 'material things' (Moore, 1925: 42) and an analysis which takes them ultimately to be identical with 'permanent possibilities of sensation' (Moore, 1925: 57), that is, mental rather than material.

Stebbing's directional analysis dispatched the issue which had so baffled Moore. On Stebbing's view, which distinguishes grammatical from metaphysical analysis, there need be nothing wrong with metaphysical analyses which have a paradoxical ring to them. Stebbing would have found this easy to see because of her years of expertise in the philosophy of physics. In Section 3.2, we saw that 'This solid table is composed of atoms which are, at the sub-atomic level, mostly empty space' has an air of paradox about it and is nevertheless true according to our best theory of physics. We do not throw out paradoxical-sounding analyses offered up by physics. We learn to live with them and distinguish them from the truisms of the language of common sense. At the level of ordinary language, 'This table is solid' does imply statements like, 'This table does not have large holes', 'This table is robust', and 'This table will bear the weight of my books'. But none of that contradicts its being mostly empty space at the subatomic level. This is a kind of directional analysis, which we rely on both in physics and in metaphysics. We do not necessarily take directional analyses to have failed if they sound paradoxical. A paradoxical-sounding definition, or a paradoxical-sounding attempt at conceptual analysis, would be problematic because those are kinds of same-level analysis. There, we often expect synonymy. In the case of directional analysis, we should not.

'This is a hand', at the level of ordinary language, implies 'This is a material object' and is incompatible with 'This is a mental object'. The latter, said of a human hand, sounds analytically false. But 'This is a hand, therefore, at the level of analysis, it is composed of permanent possibilities of sensation' should be allowed as a candidate directional analysis and not written off merely because it sounds paradoxical. Stebbing would again have explained away the air of paradoxicality as relying on a by now familiar fallacy. Just as we cannot say that 'if *men are numerous* and *Socrates is a man*, it would follow that *Socrates is numerous*' (Stebbing, 1933a: 505), we similarly cannot infer from 'This is a hand' and 'This hand is a logical construction out of permanent possibilities of sensation' that the hand is a permanent possibility of sensation, and hence a mental rather than a material object.

The analytic philosopher can no longer rest content with what Stebbing called a 'constructed deductive' system (Stebbing, 1932–3: 68) of metaphysics, one which starts from axioms taken to be necessarily true and derives theorems from those axioms using logical rules of deduction, for we no longer have a grip on necessary truth. Our certainty that some truths are self-evident was demolished by the advent of unintuitive systems such as transfinite arithmetic, infinitary set theory, and non-Euclidean geometry, and the unintuitive consequences of the new physics. Metaphysics in the twentieth century must rest on a basis of a posteriori truths. What these a posteriori truths are, and how we know about them, is a fraught question according to Stebbing.

Stebbing's metaphysical analysis presupposed a metaphysics of levels: levels of logical construction. Ordinary-language assertions are generally about logical constructs – humans, dogs, roses, tables – and their properties. Correspondence theorists say that a true sentence or proposition corresponds to a fact. But these facts themselves admit of analysis; macro-facts, like macro-physical objects, are logical constructs. The philosopher does not decompose facts themselves, but aims to arrive, by successive steps of analysis, at ever simpler facts: to 'determine the elements and the mode of combination of those elements to which reference is made when any given true assertion is made' (Stebbing, 1932–3: 79).

Stebbing also called metaphysical analysis 'directional analysis' because it has a direction: it tends towards ever greater simplicity. It descends down the levels of logical construction, in the direction of the simplest kinds of fact. The logical atomists, Russell and Moore, and by this time also Wittgenstein, were engaged in a foundationalist project, in the sense that, for the foundationalist, our knowledge of the world derives from knowledge of its individually knowable constituents. In this sense of 'foundationalist', what is known need not be mental (it may be physical or a universal), but it needs to be such that our minds can reach out and grasp it. The young Russell and Moore had insisted, against the idealists, that reality certainly is composed of mind-independent, individually cognisable, individuals in some arrangement and that these individuals and their arrangements are knowable by us. If they in turn endlessly decompose into further arrangements, we cannot be sure that we truly have grasped an individually cognisable chunk of reality. As Stebbing put it, on this view 'There must be something directly presented, otherwise there would be an infinite, vicious, regress' (1932–33: 71). So, the logical atomist must be a strong foundationalist: they must believe that analysis terminates in what Stebbing called 'basic facts' (Stebbing, 1932–33: 80; Stebbing, 1934c: 34), namely facts whose elements are simples, unconfigured elements. The lowest level is the level of simples. Higher levels have increasingly greater complexity. Grammatical analysis is 'analysis at the same level' (Stebbing, 1932–33: 77) because it links sentences to other sentences. Sentences are themselves high-level logical constructs, namely linguistic types: 'the type is a logical construction out of tokens having similarity or conventional association' (Stebbing, 1935: 9).[5] Grammatical analysis, then, links high-level logical constructs to logical constructs of the same level. It does not aim to explicate the analysandum in terms of a much simpler analysans. But directional, metaphysical, analysis must. And the logical atomist in particular must believe in analysis which terminates in an ultimate level of basic facts.

That there is an ultimate level of basic facts is, as Stebbing noted, not logically true. It is not logically true because it can be coherently denied. The statements 'There are no basic facts' or 'Analysis has no stopping

---

[5] For more on Stebbing's metaphysics of language, see Wetzel (2018).

point' are not self-contradictory. Towards the end of her paper, Stebbing concluded, 'When we have made explicit what is entailed by directional analysis, we find we must make assumptions which so far from being certainly justified, are not even very plausible' (Stebbing, 1932–33: 91–2). That there are simple, unconfigured elements which enter into basic facts is a major metaphysical assumption about the nature and structure of the world. It is not a logical truth; it may be false.

The further epistemological claim that the basic facts are also knowable by us is, similarly, at best an a posteriori truth. It is not only not necessarily true but it may easily be actually false. The logical atomist who also endorses Russell's statement that 'Every proposition which we can understand must be composed wholly of constituents with which we are acquainted' (Russell, 1910–11: 117) makes an even stronger claim than the above. Such a logical atomist makes the claim that simples are not just knowable by us but known by acquaintance, directly, without intermediary. This last claim is the one Stebbing seems to have regarded as the least plausible.

Stebbing explained that 'Russell . . . sought to discover a simple fact, which he could regard as an indubitable datum' (Stebbing, 1933b: 503). This turned out to be 'the sense-datum . . . with regard to [which] doubt is impossible . . . sense-data are to be regarded as data in simple facts' (Stebbing, 1933b: 503). But Stebbing did not think that philosophy and physics should take sense-data as a point of departure. As we saw in Section 3.1, Stebbing thought that both the philosopher and the physicist had to start from a basis of 'perceptual science', which included not just '(1) I am now seeing a red patch' but also '(2) I am now perceiving a piece of blotting paper' and '(6) Other people besides myself have seen that piece of blotting paper' (Stebbing, 1929, 147). While (1) may be indubitable, (2) and (6) are not; (2) describes a physical object, and (6) other minds. Russell regarded belief in physical objects and other minds as 'a risky inference' standing in need of justification (Stebbing, 1933b: 504). But Stebbing saw no need for an indubitable basis for philosophy. After all, she viewed philosophy as having the same observational basis of physics and took it to be obvious that the presuppositions of physics included the existence of extra-mental entities and other minds. 'The problem is not one of justifying an inference; it is a problem of analysis. We must not start from sense-data; we must start from the perceptual judgment' (Stebbing, 1932–33: 72). Stebbing saw no need for analysis to terminate in basic facts containing sense-data, nor did she think that our process of analysing a sentence must start from the consideration of sense-data. Although Stebbing regularly presented this anti-foundationalist point as disagreement with Russell, it also constitutes, to a lesser extent, disagreement with Moore. All of Moore's analyses of 'This is a hand' in 'Defence of Common Sense' start with 'This is part of the surface of a human hand', which Moore called 'undoubtedly a proposition about the sense-datum, which I am seeing' (Moore, 1925: 55).

It may be that Stebbing's expertise in the philosophy of physics enabled her to see clearly how problematic the assumption is that we have direct epistemic access to unconfigured elements of basic facts. According to our current best theory of physics, the simples are sub-atomic particles: quarks, and leptons such as electrons. But we cannot observe electrons directly. This difficulty is not a matter of our ignorance or issues with our measuring equipment which we can rectify. It is a matter of physics: to try to observe an electron, we must shine light on it, but the electron is smaller than the wavelength of visible light (Stebbing, 1937: 181). Hence there are at least some candidate simples which we cannot even in principle observe directly.

Stebbing's metaphysics, then, retained some aspects of logical atomism but dropped its strongly foundationalist assumptions. She moved towards a modest, empirically informed foundherentism which made room for the more holist Quinean and late Wittgensteinian strands of analytic philosophy which were soon to become dominant (Janssen-Lauret, 2017: 14–16). Stebbing took the view that metaphysical analysis has a legitimate role in philosophy, but whether there are basic facts, what the basic facts are, and how we know them, are all a posteriori. She was not a follower of Moore but rather an original, transitional figure who played a pivotal role in moving analytic philosophy on from its early phase – in particular the logical atomist phase of one tributary of analytic philosophy – towards a more holist middle phase. Stebbing's style of metaphysical analysis, I conclude, by contrast to Moore's, has a versatility and empiricist orientation which allows us to read her as a foremother of later, empirically informed, analytic metaphysics. Stebbing's views on metaphysics, as well as her sensitivity to ordinary language, point the way to middle and later analytic philosophy.

5 Critical Thinking and Politics

As the 1930s progressed, Stebbing felt increasingly horrified by the rise of fascism and Nazism. Stebbing supported Jewish colleagues in finding academic employment (Körber, 2019) and, with her friends and sister, took in Jewish refugee children at their school. Chapman (2013: 159) cites a letter from 1940, at which point more than fifty Jewish refugee pupils studied at the school. Feeling that she must do more, Stebbing turned her mind to the intersection of politics and what we would now call informal logic, or critical thinking. Apart from the very pressing problem of giving people the analytical tools to resist Nazism, fascism, and related ideologies, Stebbing also felt that the public ought to be given the intellectual resources to detect and overcome attempts made by politicians, journalists and newspaper editors, religious authorities, advertisements, and propaganda to manipulate them through fallacious argument or misleading uses of language.

Stebbing's *Thinking to Some Purpose* was not an academic work – in the 1930s there was not yet a recognised academic discipline of informal logic – but a book accessible to the general public. It was not the first such book; it was not even the first such book by Susan Stebbing, who had published *Logic in Practice* in 1934. Thouless's *Straight and Crooked Thinking* preceded both and also aimed to teach the general public about good reasoning. Yet Stebbing's book was highly innovative and proved very popular, in part because of her determination to provide examples of real reasoning, argument, rhetoric, and persuasion, taken from political speeches, journalism, letters to newspaper editors, and advertising. To the present day, many critical thinking textbooks still attempt to teach students to recognise good and bad reasoning based only on artificial, invented examples. Stebbing was ahead of her time, as a pre-1950s analytic philosopher, in paying close attention to ordinary usage and taking great care to supply and analyse ordinary-language examples in her work on critical thinking and politics. Her view of thinking as an activity, engaged in by humans tied to a particular culture, language, and intellectual climate was innovative, too. She aimed to teach the public to engage in goal-directed reasoning, recognise and learn to circumvent their biases, and gain an awareness of when they were being persuaded or manipulated by sham reasoning or by merely rhetorical devices. Her goal was not to persuade the population of her own views but to empower the voting public to think for themselves and to promote 'the urgent need for a democratic people to think clearly without the distortions due to unconscious bias and unrecognized ignorance' (Stebbing, 1939: 5).

We saw in Section 2.1 that, for an early analytic philosopher, Stebbing was unusually alert to the view of reasoning as an activity, engaged in by human persons who have their own distinctive personalities, speak a particular language, have a certain set of background beliefs or body of knowledge, and live in a specific cultural and intellectual climate. In modern parlance, Stebbing's reasoners are socially situated.

Even in her earliest works on logic, Stebbing wrote that the scientist 'does not always achieve – even in his published writings – that impersonality of thought which is necessary for exactness of statement. Moreover, no thinker, not even the physicist, is wholly independent of the context of experience provided for him by the society within which he works' (Stebbing, 1930: 16). In *Philosophy and the Physicists*, she criticised Eddington and Jeans for speaking as though pronouncements came straight from science itself. Stebbing objected,

> Science is not a goddess or a woman. We cannot ask science, but only scientists. Moreover, we must ask our questions of the scientist at a moment when he is in a scientific temper, capable of giving us 'the ascertained facts and provisional hypotheses' without any admixture of the emotional significance which he reads into these facts in his least scientific moods. (Stebbing, 1937: 16)

It was in *Logic in Practice* that she first wrote, 'thinking is an activity of the whole personality' (Stebbing, 1934a: vii). In *Thinking to Some Purpose*, variations on this statement recur multiple times (Stebbing, 1939: 19, 32, 35, 100, 186).

> At this point we need to remember that it is persons who think, and, therefore, persons who argue. *I* think, not something thinks in me. My intellect does not function apart from the rest of my personality. This is a statement about all thinking beings... from infancy upwards

we are forming habits, reacting to situations, experiencing emotions of various kinds; we are being constantly affected by the beliefs and modes of behaviour of those belonging to the various groups with which we have contact. (Stebbing, 1939: 32)

Stebbing consistently described reasoning as an activity and a goal-directed activity. She contrasted thinking, and reasoning, with the kind of mental activity which consists in idle reverie or free association of thought. Stebbing was concerned with the sense of 'thinking' 'in which "to think" means "to think logically"' (Stebbing, 1930: 5). This kind of thinking is purposive and goal-directed. 'Thinking is an activity. We think in order to do.... The distinction between what is often called practical thinking and theoretical thinking lies wholly in the purpose for which the thinking is pursued. In both cases the thinking process is the same; it is purposive, and thus directed' (Stebbing, 1934a: 1–2). Political action, according to Stebbing, was not a wholly separate category from reasoning but continuous with it and dependent to a large extent on good habits of thought. She wrote,

But what can we *do*? This is the question that is likely to be asked by those who are at all sensitive to the avoidable suffering that is being endured to-day through-out the world... in a time of such stress, it is nevertheless worth while for us to overhaul our mental habits, to attempt to find reasons for our beliefs, and to subject our assumptions to rigorous criticisms... A person who is called upon thus to act is more likely to act fortunately the more he has previously meditated upon actions of a similar kind. (Stebbing, 1939: 18)

Thinking, according to Stebbing, is not merely an activity but 'an activity of the whole personality' (see also Pickel, 2022). She interpreted 'personality' broadly. It included elements of culture, common knowledge held in that culture, and general intellectual climate, a person's job (Stebbing, 1939: 35) as well as what are more conventionally called personality traits, such as honesty or dishonesty (Stebbing, 1939: 82), confidence or lack of confidence (Stebbing, 1939: 99), charisma versus lack of charisma (Stebbing, 1939: 99), and being practically oriented or not (Stebbing, 1939: 42). Perhaps influenced by her reading of Aristotle, Stebbing appears to have thought of personality traits as not fixed but shaped by habit. Habits may be individual or collective, instilled by someone's work, newspaper reading, or engagement with their religious community or by their whole culture. No person is without habits of thought and 'emotional tendencies' (Stebbing, 1939: 33), nor without views shaped to an extent by their wider culture. Habits shaped by culture can be positive, for example when a teacher can 'create those mental habits that will enable his students, or pupils, to seek knowledge and to acquire the ability to form their own independent judgment based upon rational grounds' (Stebbing, 1939: 89). Still, some habits tend in the opposite direction: our cultures may lead us astray or tempt us towards mental habits which are 'lazy' (Stebbing, 1939: 92). But by teaching ourselves good habits of reasoning, we can learn to overcome any lazy, dishonest, or overly emotional cultural conditioning, as well as learn to dispense with stale habits of thought which do not serve us well.

Among Stebbing's examples of inculcating good habits of reasoning in oneself is to recognise the fallacy of special pleading: to endorse a general principle but refuse to apply it to some particular case, especially one's own case. Stebbing quoted from a letter to *The Times* by a Dr Lyttleton, who argues that poverty is good for children: 'they learn by ten years of age that there is more joy in service than in sweets; more interest in the welfare of others than in their own' (Dr Lyttleton, *The Times*, 7 October 1936, quoted in Stebbing, 1939: 45). Stebbing commented,

> You will probably have guessed that he is a man who has not himself been brought up in a poor family . . . Does he seriously believe – we should ask him – that it would have been a moral advantage to his own family had he been poor? If he assents, then he ought in consistency to wish that he had given up his income, worked hard for a low wage, and lived in a poor, over-crowded neighbourhood. If, on the contrary, he is unwilling to apply the principle to the case of his own family, then he has fallen into a serious logical confusion . . . A safeguard against this mistake is to change *you* into *I*. (Stebbing, 1939: 45–6)

Here, Stebbing can be found recommending to the reader the mental habit of checking whether they would feel the same about a given situation if they imagine it applying to themselves instead of others.

Special pleading can also take place at the level of subcultures, or whole cultures, rather than individuals. Here, it may often be more difficult to change a plural *you*, or a *they*, into a *we* if much of a person's culture represents a certain point of view and they are not exposed to the alternatives, Stebbing wrote, 'I have noticed that some Englishmen are much surprised to hear that some intelligent and not markedly Fascist Italians hold that a reasonable justification can be made out for the Italian invasion of Abyssinia' (Stebbing, 1939: 21). She also drily noted, 'Few newspapers report the opinions of foreigners about British policy, unless that opinion happens to be favourable' (Stebbing, 1939: 84). Stebbing recommended the habits of reading a broad range of different newspapers, since they will often include little discussion of opposing points of view to their prevailing political positions (Stebbing, 1939: 84) and will devote much more space to topics based on their politics (Stebbing, 1939: 223). But she recognised that formation and scrutiny of individual habits, for this problem, provided only a partial fix. She further recommended the more overtly political solution to consider 'our dependence upon newspapers for supplying us with information about what happens in the world' (Stebbing, 1939: 81) and their divided loyalties given how many newspapers are in the hands of a very few people and their aim 'to pay large dividends to . . . share-holders' (Stebbing, 1939: 82). She concluded that 'editors and journalists for the most part do very little to help us to develop habits of critical thinking' (Stebbing, 1939: 87).

Among other habits we can overcome is being taken in by 'potted thinking', that is, distilling complex thought down to simplistic slogans, and by overtly emotional or subtly emotionally charged language. Examples of potted thinking include reducing Freud's system to the slogan 'Everything is sex' (Stebbing, 1939: 65) and the anti-taxation slogan 'Food taxes mean dear food', to which Stebbing objected, 'whether food is dear or not depends partly upon the increase in real wages and in the purchasing power of money. This potted statement is likely to close the minds of unthinking or of ignorant people to any argument in favour of imposing taxes upon food, since no one wants to have dear food' (Stebbing, 1939: 64). By teaching ourselves to think through what follows from a statement of this sort, we can learn to resist 'potted thinking'. We learn the habit of putting to the test whether a slogan makes sense when we unpack it.

Stebbing took a nuanced view concerning the role of emotion in reasoning, as we would expect from someone who believes that we think with our whole personality. Stebbing emphasised that 'enthusiasm is not necessarily an enemy of thinking clearly' (Stebbing, 1939: 29) and that 'We are not purely rational beings' (Stebbing, 1939: 30). She explained, 'I do not in the least wish to suggest that it is undesirable for us to be set on thinking by emotional considerations... it is not emotion that annihilates the capacity to think clearly, but the urge to establish a conclusion in harmony with the emotion and regardless of the evidence' (Stebbing, 1939: 33). Appeals to emotion, nevertheless, may lead us away from reasoning in subtle and very unsubtle ways. Among the subtler ways are constant use of positively charged words for our own side, or the side we favour, and negatively charged words for the opposing side. Stebbing cited with approval research by Julian Huxley on language used by *The Times* for participants in the Spanish Civil War. The right-wing government and the socialist rebellion were labelled respectively as 'Referring to the Spanish Government: Loyal, Spanish, Spanish Government, Republican, Anti-Fascist, Communist. Referring to their opponents: Revolt, Insurrection, Fascist, Anti-Government, "Rebel".' Stebbing subjoined, 'You will notice, for instance, that by putting "Rebel" (in inverted commas) there is conveyed the implication that the opponents were a legitimate party engaged in a non-rebellious struggle' (Stebbing, 1939: 59–60). Emotional language may, by contrast, at times be very unsubtle and outright aim to subvert our powers of reasoning. Stebbing quoted some antisemitic hate speech by Oswald Mosley and noted that, while she 'very much dislike[d]' it, it was, in a certain sense, effective at achieving its goal of arousing emotion, as he 'sought to be offensive'. Nevertheless, she concluded, his 'habit of using strongly toned language does make for twisted thinking' (Stebbing, 1939: 57).

Stebbing maintained that speakers have a responsibility to moderate their use of persuasive devices which persuade not through convincing reasoning but by other means (Stebbing, 1939: 100). Among these devices, she counted not merely fallacious reasoning, inappropriate simplification, economic power, or inappropriate appeal to emotion but also a charismatic personality. Stebbing clearly included among the persuasive devices the cheap tricks of overconfident presentation. She wrote, 'when anyone begins an argument with such a remark as "It is indisputably true that", "Everyone knows that" or "No reasonable man can doubt that" then the people addressed may be sure that the speaker has taken for granted what he is about to assert' (Stebbing, 1939: 35). But Stebbing went further and also included speakers naturally possessed of 'a commanding presence, a fine voice and expressive gestures' as thereby having access to persuasive devices which did not convince by reason alone. She cautioned that such a speaker 'must be especially careful not to adopt a commanding manner and confident tone of voice when he is putting forward a statement which he knows to be extremely doubtful. In short, such a speaker would seem to be under an especial obligation to refrain from exploiting his personality; and subduing his hearers without convincing them' (Stebbing, 1939: 99).

Through cultivating habits of good reasoning, Stebbing believed that we could overcome our ingrained biases, conscious and unconscious. She made repeated use of the language of virtue and vice in this connection, exhorting her readers to 'scrutinize their reasoning with sufficient care' (Stebbing, 1939: 38). Aware that all humans have biases of sorts, Stebbing took pains to disclose her own to her readership. She wrote, for example, 'I may be doing Mr Ervine an injustice but I have the impression that he is a man with a mission, so that his articles are primarily intended to induce his readers to agree with him' (Stebbing, 1939: 44) and 'I personally disapprove of Sir Oswald Mosley's intention' (Stebbing, 1939: 45). In doing so, she aimed to demonstrate to the reader what the process of belief revision and good habit formation in action could look like:

> I have myself strong opinions on some of the topics that I cite as examples; I do not hope to succeed in escaping bias either in my selection or in my exposition of these examples. I should like to be able to do so, but I am aware that on many questions of practical importance I hold views that seem to me so definitely correct that I am unable to

believe that those who differ from me thereon have seen clearly what I see. (Stebbing, 1939: 54)

6 Conclusion

Susan Stebbing was not merely a disciple of G. E. Moore or an author of popular books and textbooks. She was a vital and influential figure within analytic philosophy from the 1920s to the 1940s and should be considered as one of its 'founding mothers'. We must get Stebbing out from under the shadow of Moore, recover her contributions, and further the perception of her as an important analytic philosopher, an original, transitional figure who moved British analytic philosophy on from an overly narrow and foundationalist logical atomism towards the holism and philosophy of language of middle analytic philosophy.

We have seen that Stebbing held original views on philosophical analysis, logical construction, and complete and incomplete symbol theory. She embraced incomplete symbol theory for its ability to make sense of negative existentials, so useful in philosophy of science as well as logic, but she demurred from Russell's and Moore's views that analysis analyses propositions or judgements, is analytically true, and terminates in sense-data. She took issue in particular with Russell's assumption that we can know the termini of analysis directly, by acquaintance. Stebbing's writings on these topics are interesting in isolation but are seen to have particular strength when we begin to consider her as a systematic philosopher in her own right, whose views in some areas of philosophy shaped her other views. For example, Stebbing's work on the philosophy of physics had brought home to her the fact that we physically cannot directly perceive certain simples such as electrons and that analyses may well be theoretically useful without being analytically true, such as the paradoxical-sounding but true analysis according to which my solid wooden desk consists at the subatomic level mostly of empty space.

Stebbing's substantial contributions to the philosophy of science, a topic of which Moore never made any serious study, put clear blue water between her and her mentor figure Moore and make apparent that she was certainly no mere disciple. Stebbing went in search of a philosophy to match the new Einsteinian physics, a topic on which she was self-taught, having been denied an education in the sciences as a Victorian girl with a disability. Her views resembled those of the philosopher of physics and logician Whitehead in that Stebbing considered secondary qualities to be part of nature, not mental additions. Yet she opposed Whitehead's event ontology and offered different arguments from his against the Bifurcation of Nature into primary and secondary qualities. In her book *Philosophy and the Physicists*, Stebbing investigated the then popular interpretation, due to the physicist Eddington, of Einsteinian physics in idealist terms. Stebbing, well-versed in paradoxical-sounding analyses in physics, saw no reason to dismiss the idealist interpretation as offending against common sense or internally contradictory. By itself, she maintained, physics does not force either an idealist or a materialist interpretation. Though agreeing with Eddington that physics does not tell us what the intrinsic natures of material things are, but only their extrinsic, structural relations, Stebbing saw no reason to infer from this structuralist knowledge the conclusion that its intrinsic nature is 'the stuff of consciousness'. As Eddington's views are currently undergoing a twenty-first-century resurgence, Stebbing's careful, measured counterarguments are of contemporary relevance as well.

Stebbing also made great advances in metaphysical analysis which, far from merely following Moore, made a distinct advance on his views. She distinguished what she called grammatical analysis or analysis at the same level, namely analysis of language in terms of further language, from metaphysical or directional analysis, which reveals what configuration of objects the world contains if a sentence is true. Stebbing maintained that same-level analysis could be analytically true or a priori. But, she argued, metaphysical analysis is not a process which we should expect to yield analytic, platitudinous, or logically necessary truths. This is the heart of Stebbing's solution to the paradox of analysis, pressed against Moore by Langford but never adequately addressed by Moore. Stebbing also put her metaphysical views to work in productive analyses of linguistic types, parts and wholes, and philosophy of physics. She deployed it to show why word-types can be said to be constituted out of word-tokens, and why the unintuitive nature of analysis in modern physics does not imply an idealist interpretation of it.

Lastly, Stebbing was a pioneer of the analysis of ordinary-language argumentation. An innovative logician who always strove to bring together the rigours of formally correct, universally applicable logic and its practical manifestations in inferences drawn by human beings living within language communities, cultures, and political contexts, Stebbing considered purposive thinking to be especially important in the political realm. In her works on critical thinking, she argued in favour of clearly laid-out moral and political values and ideals and above all for the paramount importance of careful analysis of political language. Many of Stebbing's social and political worries remain pertinent today. Her careful consideration of ordinary-language examples and pragmatic attention to habits of reasoning retain their relevance and have much to teach us in the twenty-first century.

References

Ayer, A. J. (1936). *Language, Truth and Logic*. London: Victor Gollancz.

Ayer, A. J. (1977). *Part of My Life*. Oxford: Oxford University Press.

Baldwin, T. (2004). 'George Edward Moore'. *Stanford Encyclopedia of Philosophy*, https://plato.stanford.edu/entries/moore/.

Barcan, R. C. (1946). 'A Functional Calculus of First Order Based on Strict Implication'. *Journal of Symbolic Logic*, 11: 1–16.

Barcan, R. C. (1947). 'The Identity of Individuals in a Strict Functional Calculus of Second Order'. *Journal of Symbolic Logic*, 12: 12–15.

Beaney, M. (2003). 'Susan Stebbing on Cambridge and Vienna Analysis'. In F. Stadler (ed.), *The Vienna Circle and Logical Empiricism*. Dordrecht: Springer, pp. 339–50.

Beaney, M. (2013). 'What Is Analytic Philosophy?' In M. Beaney (ed.) *The Oxford Handbook of Analytic Philosophy*. Oxford: Oxford University Press.

Beaney, M. (2016). 'Susan Stebbing and the Early Reception of Logical Empiricism in Britain'. In F. Stadler (ed.), *Influences on the Aufbau*. Cham: Springer, pp. 233–56.

Beaney, M. & Chapman, S. (2021). 'Susan Stebbing'. *Stanford Encyclopedia of Philosophy*, https://plato.stanford.edu/entries/stebbing/.

Bosanquet, B. (1888). 'The Philosophical Importance of a True Theory of Identity'. *Mind*, 51: 356–69.

Bradley, F. H. (1883). *The Principles of Logic*. Oxford: Oxford University Press.

Bradley, F. H. (1897). *Appearance and Reality*. London: Allen and Unwin.

Broad, C. D. (1938). Review of *Philosophy and the Physicists* by L. S. Stebbing. *Philosophy*, 13: 221–6.

Burge, T. (2005). *Truth, Thought, Reason: Essays on Frege*. Oxford: Oxford University Press.

Candlish, S. (2007). *The Russell–Bradley Dispute*. Basingstoke: Palgrave.

Carlson, S. J. (1992). 'Black Ideals of Womanhood in the Late Victorian Era'. *Journal of Negro History*, 77: 61–73.

Chapman, S. (2013). *Susan Stebbing and the Language of Common Sense*. Basingstoke: Palgrave.

Coliva, A. (2021). 'Stebbing, Moore (and Wittgenstein) on Common Sense and Metaphysical Analysis'. *British Journal for the History of Philosophy*, 29: 914–34.

Connell, S. & Janssen-Lauret, F. (2022). 'Lost Voices: On Counteracting Exclusion of Women from Histories of Contemporary Philosophy'. *British Journal for the History of Philosophy*, 30: 199–210.

Connell, S. & Janssen-Lauret, F. (in press). '"Bad Philosophy" or "Derivative Philosophy": Labels That Keep Women Out of the Canon'. *Metaphilosophy*.

Douglas, A. X. and Nassim, J. (2021). 'Susan Stebbing's Logical Interventionism'. *History and Philosophy of Logic*, 42: 101–17.

Eddington, A. (1920). *Space, Time, and Gravitation*. Cambridge: Cambridge University Press.

Eddington, A. (1928). *The Nature of the Physical World*. New York: Macmillan.

Frege, G. (1879). *Begriffsschrift: Eine der arithmetischen nachgebildete Formelsprache des reinen Denkens*. Halle: Louis Nebert.

Hopkins, A. (1913). 'Some Ideals of the Suffrage Shattered by Searching Analysis'. *The Woman's Protest*, 2: 3–8.

Hylton, P. (1990). *Russell, Idealism, and the Emergence of Analytic Philosophy*. Oxford: Clarendon.

Janssen-Lauret, F. (2022a). 'Susan Stebbing's Metaphysics and the Status of Common-Sense Truths'. In J. Peijnenburg & S. Verhaegh (eds.), *Women in the History of Analytic Philosophy*. Cham: Springer, pp. 169–92.

Janssen-Lauret, F. (2022b). 'Ruth Barcan Marcus and Quantified Modal Logic'. *British Journal for the History of Philosophy*, 30: 353–83.

Janssen-Lauret, F. (2022c). 'Women in Logical Empiricism'. In T. Uebel & C. Limbeck-Lilienau (eds.), *The Routledge Handbook of Logical Empiricism*. London: Routledge, pp. 127–35.

Janssen-Lauret, F. (2018). 'W. V. Quine's Philosophical Development in the 1930s and 1940s'. In W. V. Quine (author) and W. Carnielli, F. Janssen-Lauret, and W. Pickering (eds.), *The Significance of the New Logic*. Cambridge: Cambridge University Press, pp. xiv–xlvii.

Janssen-Lauret, F. (2017). 'Susan Stebbing, Incomplete Symbols, and Foundherentist Meta-Ontology'. *Journal for the History of Analytical Philosophy*, 5: 6–17.

Janssen-Lauret, F. (in press-a). 'Grandmothers of Analytic Philosophy'. In R. Cook & A. Yap (eds.), *Feminist Philosophy and Formal Logic*, Vol. 20, Minnesota Studies in Philosophy of Science. Minneapolis: University of Minnesota Press.

Janssen-Lauret, F. (in press-b). 'Grace de Laguna As a Grandmother of Analytic Philosophy'. *Australasian Philosophical Review*.

Janssen-Lauret, F. (in press-c). 'Grandmothers and Founding Mothers of Analytic Philosophy: Constance Jones, Bertrand Russell, and Susan Stebbing on Complete and Incomplete Symbols'. In L. Elkind & A. Klein (eds.), *Russell and Women*. London: Palgrave.

Johnson, W. E. (1921–4). *Logic*, Vols. 1–3. Cambridge: Cambridge University Press.

Jones, C. (2000). 'Grace Chisholm Young: Gender and Mathematics around 1900'. *Women's History Review*, 9: 675–93.

Jones, E. E. C. (1890). *Elements of Logic As a Science of Propositions*. Edinburgh: T. and T. Clark.

Jones, E. E. C. (1892). *An Introduction to General Logic*. London: Longmans, Green, and Co.

Jones, E. E. C. (1900–01). 'The Meaning of Sameness'. *Proceedings of the Aristotelian Society* 1: 167–173.

Jones, E. E. C. (1905). *A Primer of Logic*. New York: E. P. Dutton.

Jones, E. E. C. (1913). *A Primer of Logic*, 2nd ed. New York: E. P. Dutton.

Jones, E. E. C. (1922). *As I Remember*. London: A. & C. Black.

Kant, I. (1787). *Kritik der reinen Vernunft*, 2nd ed. Translated (1929) *Critique of Pure Reason*, ed. and trans. N. Kemp Smith. New York: St. Martin's Press.

Katzav, J. & Vaesen, K. (2017). 'On the Emergence of American Analytic Philosophy'. *British Journal for the History of Philosophy*, 25: 772–98.

Klein, A. (1911). 'Negation Considered As a Statement of Difference in Identity'. *Mind*, 20: 521–9.

Körber, S. (2019). 'Thinking about the Common Reader: Neurath, Stebbing and the Modern Picture-Text Style'. In J. Cat &

A. T. Tuboly (eds.), *Neurath Reconsidered*. Cham: Springer, pp. 451–70.

Ladd, C. (1883). 'On the Algebra of Logic'. In C. S. Peirce (ed.), *Studies in Logic, by Members of the Johns Hopkins University*. Boston, MA: Little, Brown & Co., pp. 17–71.

Ladd-Franklin, C. (1889). 'On Some Characteristics of Symbolic Logic'. *The American Journal of Psychology*, 2: 543–67.

Ladd-Franklin, C. (1911). 'The Foundations of Philosophy Explicit Primitives'. *Journal of Philosophy, Psychology and Scientific Methods*, 8: 708–13.

Ladd-Franklin, C. (1912). 'Implication and Existence in Logic'. *The Philosophical Review*, 21: 641–65.

Ladd-Franklin, C. (1928). 'The Antilogism'. *Mind*, 37: 532–4.

Langford, C. H. (1942). 'The Notion of Analysis in Moore's Philosophy'. In P. Schilpp (ed.), *The Philosophy of G. E. Moore*. La Salle, IL: Open Court, pp. 321–42.

Laslett, B. & Brenner, J. (1989). 'Gender and Social Reproduction: Historical Perspectives'. *Annual Review of Sociology*, 15: 381–404.

MacBride, F. (2018). *On the Genealogy of Universals*. Oxford: Oxford University Press.

MacBride, F. & Janssen-Lauret, F. (2015). 'Meta-Ontology, Epistemology, and Essence: On the Empirical Deduction of the Categories'. *The Monist*, 98: 290–302.

Mercier, C. (1915). 'Logic: A Rejoinder to Miss Stebbing'. *Science Progress in the Twentieth Century*, 10: 17–26.

Milkov, N. (2003). 'Susan Stebbing's Criticism of Wittgenstein's *Tractatus*'. In F. Stadler (ed.), *The Vienna Circle and Logical Empiricism*. Dordrecht: Springer, pp. 351–63.

Mill, J. S. (1884 [1843]). *A System of Logic*. London: Longmans.

Moore, G. E. (1899). 'The Nature of Judgement'. *Mind*, 8: 176–93.

Moore, G. E. (1900–01). 'Identity'. *Proceedings of the Aristotelian Society*, 1: 103–27.

Moore, G. E. (1903). 'The Refutation of Idealism'. *Mind*, 12: 433–53.

Moore, G. E. (1925). 'A Defence of Common Sense'. In J. Muirhead (ed.), *Contemporary British Philosophy*, reprinted in Moore's

1959 *Philosophical Papers*, London: George Allen and Unwin, pp. 32–59.

Naden, C. (1890). *Induction and Deduction*. London: Bickers.

Passmore, J. (1966). *A Hundred Years of Philosophy*, 2nd ed. London: Penguin.

Paul, G. A. (1938). Review of *Philosophy and the Physicists* by L. S. Stebbing. *Mind*, 47: 361–76.

Pickel, B. (2022). 'Susan Stebbing's Intellectualism'. *Journal for the History of Analytical Philosophy*, 10: 1–24.

Quine, W. V. (1953). 'Reference and Modality'. In *From a Logical Point of View*, Cambridge, MA: Harvard University Press.

Quine, W. V. (2018 [1944]). *The Significance of the New Logic*. Cambridge: Cambridge University Press.

Quinton, A. (2005). 'Analytic Philosophy'. In T. Honderich (ed.), *Oxford Handbook of Philosophy*, 2nd ed. Oxford: Oxford University Press, p. 28.

Russell, B. (1903). *The Principles of Mathematics*. Cambridge: Cambridge University Press.

Russell, B. (1910–11). 'Knowledge by Acquaintance and Knowledge by Description'. *Proceedings of the Aristotelian Society*, 11: 108–28.

Russell, B. (1919). *Introduction to Mathematical Philosophy*. London: George Allen and Unwin.

Russell, B. (1926). Review of Ogden and Richards, *The Meaning of Meaning*. *The Dial*, 81: 114–121.

Shen, E. (1927). 'The Ladd-Franklin Formula in Logic: The Antilogism'. *Mind*, 36: 54–60.

Soames, S. (2003). *The Dawn of Analysis, Vol. 1: Philosophical Analysis in the Twentieth Century*. Princeton, NJ: Princeton University Press.

Stebbing, L. S. (1914). *Pragmatism and French Voluntarism*. Cambridge: Cambridge University Press.

Stebbing, L. S. (1915). 'A Reply to Some Charges Against Logic'. *Science Progress in the Twentieth Century*, 9: 406–12.

Stebbing, L. S. (1916–17). 'Relation and Coherence'. *Proceedings of the Aristotelian Society*, 17: 459–80.

Stebbing, L. S. (1917–18). 'The Philosophical Importance of the Verb "To Be" '. *Proceedings of the Aristotelian Society*, 18: 582–9.

Stebbing, L. S. (1924). 'Mind and Nature in Prof. Whitehead's Philosophy'. *Mind*, 33: 289–303.

Stebbing, L. S. (1924–5). 'Universals and Professor Whitehead's Theory of Objects'. *Proceedings of the Aristotelian Society*, 25: 305–30.

Stebbing, L. S. (1926). 'Professor Whitehead's "Perceptual Object" '. *Journal of Philosophy*, 23: 197–213.

Stebbing, L. S. (1927). 'Abstraction and Science'. *Journal of Philosophical Studies*, 2: 309–22.

Stebbing, L. S. (1928). 'Materialism in the Light of Modern Scientific Thought'. *Proceedings of the Aristotelian Society* Suppl. 8: 112–61.

Stebbing, L. S. (1929). 'Realism and Modern Physics'. *Proceedings of the Aristotelian Society*, Suppl. 9: 112–61.

Stebbing, L. S. (1929–30). 'Concerning Substance'. *Proceedings of the Aristotelian Society*, 30: 285–308.

Stebbing, L. S. (1930). *A Modern Introduction to Logic*, 1st ed. London: Methuen.

Stebbing, L. S. (1932). 'Substances, Events and Facts'. *Journal of Philosophy*, 29: 309–22.

Stebbing, L. S. (1932–33). 'The Method of Analysis in Metaphysics'. *Proceedings of the Aristotelian Society*, 33: 65–94.

Stebbing, L. S. (1933a). *A Modern Introduction to Logic*, 2nd ed. London: Methuen.

Stebbing, L. S. (1933b). *Logical Positivism and Analysis*. London: H. Milford.

Stebbing, L. S. (1933–34). 'Constructions: The Presidential Address'. *Proceedings of the Aristotelian Society*, 34: 1–30.

Stebbing, L. S. (1933c). 'The "A Priori" '. *Proceedings of the Aristotelian Society*. Suppl. 12: 178–97.

Stebbing, L. S. (1933d). 'Mr. Joseph's Defence of Free Thinking in Logistics'. *Mind*, 42: 338–51.

Stebbing, L. S. (1934a). *Logic in Practice.* London: Methuen.

Stebbing, L. S. (1934b). 'Communication and Verification'. *Proceedings of the Aristotelian Society*, Suppl. 13: 159–73.

Stebbing, L. S. (1934c). 'Directional Analysis and Basic Facts'. *Analysis*, 2: 33–6.

Stebbing, L. S. (1935). 'Sounds, Shapes and Words'. *Proceedings of the Aristotelian Society*, Suppl. 14: 1–21.

Stebbing, L. S. (1937). *Philosophy and the Physicists*. London: Penguin.

Stebbing, L. S. (1938–9). 'Some Puzzles about Analysis'. *Proceedings of the Aristotelian Society*, 39: 69–84.

Stebbing, L. S. (1939). *Thinking to Some Purpose*. London: Penguin.

Stebbing, L. S. (1942). 'Moore's Influence'. In P. Schilpp (ed.), *The Philosophy of G. E. Moore*. La Salle, IL: Open Court, pp. 515–32.

Stebbing, L. S. (1942–3). 'The New Physics and Metaphysical Materialism'. *Proceedings of the Aristotelian Society*, 43: 167–214.

Stout, G. F. (1922). 'The Late Miss E. E. Constance Jones'. *Mind*, 31: 385–412.

Tarski, A. (1956 [1935]). ' Uber die Beschränktheit der Ausdrucksmittel deduktiver Theorien'. *Ergebnisse eines mathematischen Kolloquiums*, 7: 15–22. Reprinted as 'On the Limitations of the Means of Expression of Deductive Theories'. In *Logic, Semantics and Metamathematics*, ed. and trans. A. Tarski & J. H. Woodger. Oxford: Oxford University Press, pp. 384–92.

Thouless, R. (1930). *Straight and Crooked Thinking*. London: Hodder & Stoughton.

Uckelman, S. L. (2021). 'What Problem Did Ladd-Franklin (Think She) Solve(d)?' *Notre Dame Journal of Formal Logic*, 62: 527–52.

Urmson, J. O. (1956). *Philosophical Analysis*. Oxford: Oxford University Press.

Venn, J. (1883). Review of *Studies in Logic*, ed. by C. S. Peirce. *Mind*, 8: 594–603.

Warnock, M. (2000). *A Memoir: People and Places*. London: Duckworth.

West, P. (2022). 'The Philosopher versus the Physicist: Susan Stebbing on Eddington and the Passage of Time'. *British Journal for the History of Philosophy*, 30: 130–51.

Wetzel, L. (2018). 'Types and Tokens'. *Stanford Encyclopedia of Philosophy*, https://plato.stanford.edu/entries/types-tokens/.

Whitehead, A. N. (1898). *A Treatise on Universal Algebra: With Applications*. Cambridge: Cambridge University Press.

Whitehead, A. N. & Russell, B. (1964 [1910]). *Principia Mathematica to *56*. Cambridge: Cambridge University Press.

Wisdom, J. (1944). 'L. Susan Stebbing'. Mind 53: 283–285

Wittgenstein, L. (1922). *Tractatus Logico-Philosophicus*. London: Kegan Paul.

Ω (1891). Review of *Induction and Deduction* by Constance Naden. *The Monist*, 1: 292–4.

Acknowledgements

Many thanks to the series editor, Jacqueline Broad, and to Sophia Connell, Siobhan Chapman, Maheshi Gunawardane, Fraser MacBride, Thomas Uebel, to audiences at the Universities of Boise State, Cambridge, Durham, Glasgow, Leiden, London, and Manchester, especially Simone Kotva, Bridger Landle, Bryan Pickel, Catherine Pickstock, Lukas Verburgt, and Peter West, and to the students in my MA History of Analytic Philosophy course and in my third-year Language and Analysis course.

Cambridge Elements ≡

Women in the History of Philosophy

Jacqueline Broad
Monash University

Jacqueline Broad is Associate Professor of Philosophy at Monash University, Australia. Her area of expertise is early modern philosophy, with a special focus on seventeenth- and eighteenth-century women philosophers. She is the author of *Women Philosophers of the Seventeenth Century* (Cambridge University Press, 2002), *A History of Women's Political Thought in Europe, 1400–1700* (with Karen Green; Cambridge University Press, 2009), and *The Philosophy of Mary Astell: An Early Modern Theory of Virtue* (Oxford University Press, 2015).

Advisory Board

About the Series
In this Cambridge Elements series, distinguished authors provide concise and structured introductions to a comprehensive range of prominent and lesser-known figures in the history of women's philosophical endeavour, from ancient times to the present day.

Cambridge Elements ≡

Women in the History of Philosophy

Elements in the Series

A full series listing is available at: www.cambridge.org/EWHP

Printed in the United States
by Baker & Taylor Publisher Services